Writers Resist

The Anthology 2018

Editors
Kit-Bacon Gressitt and Sara Marchant

Running Wild Press
Los Angeles

Text copyright © 2018 Running Wild Press

Cover image is from the painting *Sisters*, © Patrick N. Brown, www.PatrickNBrown.net.

Published in North America and Europe by Running Wild Press. Visit Running Wild Press at www.runningwildpress.com Educators, librarians, book clubs (as well as the eternally curious), go to www.runningwildpress.com for teaching tools.

ISBN 978-1-947041-13-4 (pbk)
ISBN 978-1-947041-14-1 (ebook)

Library of Congress Control Number 2018939857
Printed in the United States of America.

Dedication

To Activist Writers

By Rachel Federman

They said, "You sounded angry." They thought this would humiliate you. Make you stop writing or change your tone to something less strident. "Anger is not becoming," they said. They did not know that anger is how you will become who you are.

"Literature is dying," they warned, shuttering up Humanities departments, shaking their heads when you said you were majoring in English. But you know literature is alive. It is a live thing, alive through you, how you breathe, bookstores your temples. You are searching for new green lights, a multicolored whale, woods of your own where you will live deliberately. "Literature is not dying," you said defiantly. "For many of us, it has only just begun."

They said, "The written word has lost its power." But that was before they saw what you wrote.

Rachel Federman is a writer and musician who lives smack dab in the middle of Manhattan, but likes to pretend she's in a small river town. She studied writing and literature at Dartmouth and holds a Master of Arts in English Literature from Fordham University. As a social justice advocate, she works to improve education outcomes for minority students through program evaluation. She writes about motherhood, nature and the imagination at Last American Childhood. Learn more about her at rachelfederman.com.

Contents

Introduction

It began on November 9, 2016, in a message, simple yet with an undercurrent of utter dismay:

"What the fuck do we do now?" Sara asked, her grief and rage overcoming her manners.

"Why are you asking me? I hardly know you." K-B wasn't ready for correspondence, having spent the previous day working a polling place giddy with Trump supporters.

"I know from our MFA program that you're an activist. I know nothing about activism, but we have to *do something*. What do we do?"

"Well, we're writers. ..."

So was born *Writers Resist*. The online literary journal launched at WritersResist.com on December 1, 2016, publishing works by writerly friends.

Then wonderful things happened.

People determined to *do something* found *Writers Resist* and sent us their stories, essays, poetry and art—from the United States and beyond. Marchers from the worldwide uprising the day after Trump's inauguration sent us their writings. An Italian graphic artist shared his concept of Trump's wall. A poet from the U.S. South bared his progressive sonnets, albeit using a pseudonym. A feminist writer in Nigeria delighted us with her short story about trouncing the patriarchy. Writers in exile declared poetic challenges to fascism. Authors and artists and teachers and gardeners and veterans and performers and lawyers and students and doctors and parents and expats, they sent their fear and shock, rage and sorrow, and their profound sense of hope.

Because they know this: Their voices are being heard; the resistance against violence, patriarchy and bigotry continues; feminism is powerful; and in solidarity we will survive and thrive.

We know this, too.

"So, what do we do now?" Sara and K-B asked each other.

So was born *Writers Resist: The Anthology 2018*. It's a representation of our first year of publishing, plus a few extras we're eager to share.

P.S. If you like what we're doing, please visit our website, at www.WritersResist.com, and sponsor a writer or artist—or two.

Violence

violence: physical or emotional force intended to silence, harm, damage or kill

state violence: violence enacted by the State or its agents that prevents people from achieving their potential, for example, the prosecution of peaceful protesters, unwarranted surveillance, institutionalized racism, deporting Dreamers, oppression of *others*, punishing the poor for being poor, inciting rhetoric from political leaders …

Left for Dead Barbie Visits the Capital, on the preceding page, is by Susan Arthur, a photographer, sculptor and writer, with an MFA from Vermont College of Fine Arts. She hides out in the very blue wilds of Massachusetts. Her work is shown nationally, and she's a member of the artist co-op Brickbottom Artists Association, in Somerville, Massachusetts. Visit her website at SusanArthur.net.

Today

By Tori Cárdenas

Today, my baby came home crying, saying, "Mama I need new shoes." As of yesterday, seventeen more people are dead. My baby came home and said, "Mama I need new shoes," and before we could ask if she was being bullied, she said,

If a shooter comes into my classroom,

and I'm wearing my light-up shoes,

they will help him find me.

Today, my baby came home crying. But she came home. Tomorrow, who knows.

Tori Cárdenas is a queer Puerto Rican poet from Albuquerque, New Mexico.

The Prescription

By Carolyn Ziel

My friend Jill posted a picture of Steve Bannon on Facebook with his quote, "Birth control makes women unattractive and crazy." Jill's comment was "Oh my God! Oh my God! Oh my God!" My response was "hash tag medical marijuana."

I was kidding when I wrote it. But on Tuesday afternoon at 4:30, as the sun skidded the sky with Caribbean color, I pulled into a strip mall in Wilmington, off Pacific Coast Highway, for an appointment to get my prescription. Five storefronts lined the parking lot. A liquor store and the medical clinic were the only two that weren't vacant, and a guy with his hands in his pockets loitered in a shadowy corner. I thought about driving away, but I got out of the car, put my purse on my shoulder and walked to a door with white block lettering: PCH Medical Clinic.

The office was cold. The walls were ghost white. My boots clicked on the dark brown parquet floors.

"Hi," I said to the twenty-something girl sitting at a desk in a small office behind a window. "I called earlier."

She looked up at me and smiled. "I've never done this before," I said. I'd googled *medical marijuana doctors*. This place had 5 1/2 stars on Yelp.

The girl gave me some forms to fill out. I checked off the symptoms anxiety, stress and insomnia, and ticked depression and back pain for good measure. I signed several waivers promising not to drive under the influence or operate heavy machinery, and not to sell, redistribute or share my marijuana.

When I gave her my completed paperwork, I noticed an ATM in the corner. "Do you take credit cards?"

"No," she said. "The appointment is $50 cash, if you have the coupon. It'll be $65 without it. You'll need cash for the dispensary, too." I got $200 from the machine.

I didn't wait more than five minutes before she called for me. As I followed her into the back I heard the ring of a Skype call. She brought me into an office with an oak desk. On it sat a computer monitor and a mouse.

"He's not here?" I said.

She wiggled the mouse, connected the call and walked out of the room, closing the door behind her. I sat down and smiled at myself in the small box at the bottom of the screen, pale in my black Equinox t-shirt. My mouth was dry. I put my purse on my lap and folded my hands over it.

"Hello," said a face on the screen. He was bald, shiny and overexposed. He wore a white lab coat and looked up at me through gold wire-framed glasses. I took him to be in his early 70s. "Can you hear me?" he asked.

"Yes, hello."

"So." He looked down at the forms twenty-something girl must have faxed to him. "How long have you had insomnia?"

"On and off for a couple of months." I lied.

"And you have some back pain?" He was writing.

"My lower back," I said. That was true, I'd just come from the chiropractor.

7

"How long have you been depressed?"

One of the definitions for depression is *low in spirits*. Another is *vertically flattened*. I felt both. My anxiety was real. But I didn't want him to think I needed a shrink and meds or I wouldn't get my weed.

I made the decision to get the prescription after a white delivery truck barreled toward me in traffic that morning. I had to swerve and jump a lane to get out of its trajectory. That's when I burst. I couldn't stop crying. The level of the swamp out there is getting high and there's a riptide pulling me out to sea. I didn't want to cry here, in front of the Skype doctor, let my guard down. I needed to be calm. Explain in a mature tone that I just needed a little soft focus.

"Here's the thing," I said. "I'm not officially depressed. It's more like I'm stressed." I paused. He kept writing. I didn't want to say the wrong thing. I wanted to be cool. "It's not like I want to be stoned all the time. I mean I heard that there's this stuff that just takes the edge off, you know, without being super stoney." My heart skipped and slipped into my stomach. I felt awkward. I looked at myself on the screen and took a breath. Tried to gather my thoughts. Stay calm.

"The truth is," I said, "this election, well, the outcome and everything has me really freaked out." Shit, I didn't mean to say that. What if he voted for the guy? He could be one of those people that says, "Hey, we put up with Obama for eight years and we survived."

A penny lay on the desk by the monitor. If a penny lands heads up, its good luck. If it's tails, I flip it over, give someone else a chance to find a little luck. I needed some luck. These days, everyone I care about, that I'm close to, can use a little luck. A little softness. A little kindness. A little ease. Luck that lets you know you'll be fine. Everything will be okay. Gives solace. The kind of luck that's light. Light like compassion, peace, hope. I reached for the penny. Tossed it. Tails. I flipped it over.

The doctor stopped writing and looked up at me. I hoped he'd give me my prescription and I could buy some liquid miracle and a vape pen. Some Acapulco gold, purple haze or amnesia. That's what I needed.

"Tell me about it," he said. "These are some crazy times." He smiled a soft smile. "You can pick up your prescription at the front desk."

"That's it?"

"Yes," he said, and the call was disconnected. I took a deep breath and exhaled for what felt like the first time in weeks.

Carolyn Ziel is a writer, workshop leader and member of Jack Grapes Los Angeles Poets & Writers Collective. Her work has appeared or is forthcoming in such journals as *Diverse Voices Quarterly*, *CRATE Literary Journal*, *Cultural Weekly*, *The Los Angeles Review of Los Angeles*, *Edgar Allen Poet*, *ONTHEBUS* and *FR&D*. She has studied with Ellen Bass, Dorianne Laux, Joseph Millar, Richard Jones and Pam Huston. Her collection of poetry, *as simple as that*, is available on Amazon. She is a regular contributor to *The Huffington Post* and *Thrive Global*.

This essay was previously published online by *Writers Resist*.

The No-Knock State

By Jemshed Khan

Upon hearing that Barrett Brown was jailed (again)

SWAT teams rumble streets.
Men in black smash down doors.

No one bothered to knock
65,000 times last year:

Hinges ripped from the jamb
with a battering ram or breach grenade.

My friend murmurs,
We live in a Police State,

but I still write and say and read
as I will, as we wait.

He points and whispers,
Someone's listening at the door.

I hiss back, *Surely. Enough. Already.*
Though I turn and look to be sure.

Jemshed Khan lives and works in the Kansas City area. Born overseas of immigrant parents, he has experienced American culture both as an outsider and as a participant. He relishes the opportunity that the American dream and society have offered him, but also is alarmed by the rising authoritarian encroachment on privacy and freedom.

This poem was previously published online by *Writers Resist.*

Turns Out

By Sam Sax

all the holocaust books we read
in grade school weren't enough.
the class outraged, youth shouting
never again. in the texts i became

brave, resistance child, stalking
the night's antique shadows, disproving
a devil's arithmetic, lettering every star.
easy to be righteous in the face

of tyranny so dead, the terror's just
an old rope of letters, a photograph
developed in a darkroom, the tattoo
on a family member's leathered arm

but even he smiles as you dance
around like the goofy animal you are.
what then when the terror lives?
when the cabinet's filled with poison bread?

when they come for my friends,
when they come to my bed, when
they come, they come. come stars
to guide our meat across the night's

opera of skulls. come letters brave
enough to harvest joy from the coming
darkness. come art sharp as a knife
tearing the blood from the white

in our flag. you can say there is no road
map for the red mattress, for the police
—bag forced over a chanting head. but look
to any history & there's the path

an outraged flood, a million bodies
in the street, a fence between blood & money,
a government shaking. for our lives & our love
we must do all we can before we're forced

back below the floorboards.

Sam Sax is the Texas-based author of *Madness* (Penguin, 2017), 2016
National Poetry Series winner, *Bury It* (Wesleyan University Press,
2018), and four chap books: *All The Rage* (Sibling Rivalry Press, 2016)
Straight (Winner of the Diode Editions Chapbook Prize, 2016) *Sad
Boy / Detective* (Winner of The Black Lawrence Chapbook Prize,
2015), and *A Guide to Undressing Your Monsters* (Button Poetry,

2014). Sam has received fellowships from the National Endowment for the Arts, Lambda Literary, and The Michener Center for Writers, where he served as the Editor-in-chief of *Bat City Review*. He has poems published or forthcoming in *Agni, American Poetry Review, Boston Review, Ploughshares, Guernica, Poetry Magazine*, and other journals. Visit his website at www.samsax.com.

This poem was previously published online by *Writers Resist*.

When You Send an Email Asking for Money to Support that Mission Bringing Jesus to Romania

By Alina Stefanescu

I was born in a land wiped clean from the maps, a place you associate with AIDS-stricken orphans, tucked into Balkans, needing your bibles. Idiots needing salvation. Peasants needing administrations of missionary impulse. Come clear-cut this culture. Plant a flag. Mail a postcard. How you would have loved Ceausescu, his staunch anti-abortion policies. The workplace vaginal exams required by law. To check women for babies. To save baby lives while denying a mother's. Illegal abortions, automated jail time. Birth control punished as contraband traffick, a violation of the national body. Borders decided the line between import and crime. Only Party members were permitted the honor of empty wombs. Only the Party ensured flesh against fetus. Pro-life is this boot on the neck of a lesser human, a blade you sanctify with statecraft.

I was born in a place where parents listened to shadows inching over concrete. Shadows don't speak unless you count subtraction—the sound sucked away from nearby objects. A woman's body is a mine, a natural resource. What's natural is owned by men. You with bona fide smiles and big ole blessings. You with holy-roller heads & empty hearts. You hear nothing. Count the silence articulated in the portrait's airbrush to taste the melody of what is missing. A math you cannot imagine. You who are blind. You who don't see foreshortened folk ambling sidewalks. Take refuge beneath a roof slant. Seek the refuge you won't grant refugees. You are busy bearing bibles. You are bringing the bible to the people of Romania. You are coming, eager to selfie. Tell the world what you've done for Romania. Tell what you've done.

I was born in a land that stopped naming its children Nicolae. The dictator's name curses any child it touches. I am in love with the vacant wist of the local executioner, his grizzled voice, mourning the retirement of Alabama's Yellow Mama. A mother who kills is a native Kali. An electric chair is the proper American matriarch, penultimate sizzle. Baptists forge petitions to bring Yellow Mama back. My mongrel womb won't bear your life. I sew lips shut, vagina muzzled, verbs safe inside. My body is forbidden samizdat. Paul Celan is my answer. Please keep your American Jesus at home. Muffle his face with flags. Stars and bars you brand across his back.

Alina Stefanescu was born in Romania, raised in Alabama, and reared by various friendly ghosts. She is a 2016 Pushcart Prize nominee for poetry, and she won the 2015 Ryan R. Gibbs Flash Fiction Award and was a finalist for the 2015 Robert Dana Poetry Award. Her poetry and prose can be found in *PoemMemoirStory*, *Shadowgraph Quarterly*, *Parcel*, *Noble Gas Quarterly*, *Minola Review*, and others. *Objects In Vases*, a poetry chapbook, was published by Anchor & Plume in March 2016. Alina currently lives in Tuscaloosa with her partner and four friendly mammals. Connect with her at www.alinastefanescu.com or on Twitter @aliner.

Author's note: Wrote it after re-reading Svetlana Alexievich and thinking how much the Russian desire for the "strong man" resembles America's. And how sad.

This essay was previously published online by *Writers Resist.*

An Old Dog Never Barks at Gunmen

By Bola Opaleke

– Neither should you,

a wise man once said. Even pickaxes
and sledgehammers would do just fine –
like pickaxe-men or sledgehammer-men.

That reminds me of people that left
raising a finger of "revenge my death" up so high

as the bullet-ridden body thuds. What the soldiers
have done to us – young girls –
teaching our heliotropic breasts how to worship the sun,

boys abandoning the fishing rods
for militants' rifles, men and women

waking up in the morning
to homelessness. A daughter defiled
before the helpless father – his body at twilight,

dangling from a rope hugging a barren tree
his wooden hands never again to cradle a crying child.

I saw a mother rubbing her frail skin with black ash
from her son's barrow, invoking spirits
of vengeance from that mound. Soldiers

picking our tiniest vein to sew up our lips –
to make us talk in pains – to force us to obey

word count. No soldiers. No! The poor *barks*
at the *Law* (that only eavesdrops). These ordinances give
different uniforms to different soldiers

at different levels of our democracy.
These soldiers, wearing different gears –

bath in "constitution of lies."
But because an old dog never barks at gunmen,
neither do we. "Raise a sword

of rebellion against thieves and murderers,"
wrote a poet," and watch politics be

white as snow." Not soaring past
the red line that says: *survive or die*
because we already fall in love

with "Que Sera Sera" –
that evergreen lyric of consolation

seeping through. Radios and televisions
propagating that wise saying every minute:
"an old dog never barks at gunmen –

neither should you."

Bola Opaleke is a Nigerian-Canadian poet residing in Winnipeg, MB. His poems have appeared or are forthcoming in *Rattle, Cleaver, One, The Nottingham Review, The Puritan, The Literary Review of Canada, Sierra Nevada Review, Dissident Voice, Poetry Quarterly, The Indianapolis Review, Miracle E-Zine, Poetry Pacific, Drunk Monkeys, League of Canadian Poets* (Poetry Month 2013), *Pastiche Magazine, The Society,* Vol. 10, 2013, St. Peter's College, University of Saskatchewan, and others. He holds a degree in City Planning. His poem was inspired by the incidents surrounding Kenya's presidential election. And the attack, arrest and imprisonment of the Catalan leaders seeking independence from Spain.

This poem was previously published online by *Writers Resist.*

Jump

By Yazmin Navarro

There was always an ache.
A pain that filled the inside of my belly.
A pain that engulfed me.
Of missing something.
Of missing someone.
Of missing my mother.

It was the times.
It was the need.
It was seeing the hunger in her children's eyes.
It was the fear of watching her children die.
She pried my hand from hers.
She looked away.
She feared my wounded face.
She didn't look back.
She feared my face more than she feared the abyss.

She didn't know how.
She didn't know when.

She didn't know where.
But she knew the answers lay ahead.
In a foreign land.
With a foreign tongue.
She could feed her children from there.
She could sustain her children from there.

She lost her children.
And I lost my mother.
Fuck you fence.
Jump.
No one wins.

Yazmin Navarro holds a BA in English and a Masters in Public Administration. She was born in Northern Mexico and immigrated to the United States as a 7-year-old. In her spare time, she writes about growing up as an undocumented immigrant—the hardships faced as a child brought to a country she didn't know and her difficult path to authorized status—and she's currently working on a children's book. Yazmin has been a Marine Corps spouse for the past twelve years, she has a daughter and two dogs, and they reside in Southern California.

This poem was previously published online by *Writers Resist*.

I Still Am

By David Martinez

I'm reading *Open Veins of Latin America*—because I'm writing *my* South-American book—when the woman in the parking lot starts to scream. The man's screaming, too, and it's violent screaming, and I can't see them. But I know they're both red-faced, and she's crying. She's shrieking. They've both been shrieking for a lifetime, but I couldn't hear them. Can only hear them now, like it's a veil been lifted.

I go to my apartment door and the noise comes in louder. The baby in the mix is wailing like he's hurt. But I stand there and peek though the cracked-open door. I don't want them to see me because I don't want them to go inside, because I don't know what apartment they live in and closed doors are more dangerous than open ones, and apartments are more dangerous than parking lots. That's what I tell myself, but maybe I'm just scared. I leave the door cracked, fall back in, and call the police. I'm terrified of police. But there's a raging man and a raging woman and a baby, and I have no power, so I *have to* call.

What's the emergency? The woman on the line says.

They're fighting outside.

•

He's my fucking child, the man says. He's my blood.

There's a slam against a car, a thud, a clamor.

•

Do you know the couple? the dispatcher asks.

No, I say. But I've seen them before.

•

The woman is pleading. The man shouts.

He calls her a cunt. He calls her a bitch. He calls her a whore.

•

Are you outside? the dispatcher says. Can you see them?

No, I say. I'm inside. But I can see the car and their heads. The guy is half in the car.

•

She sobs. She pleads. She yells, Get the fuck out of my car! You're not right. Please, please get the fuck out of my car.

Another drunk thud and a splatter.

Yeah, he yells. Swing at me! Swing at me! I dare you, you fucking bitch. Think I won't swing back?

No! No, please! I have a baby in my arms.

•

Sir, they're next to what kind of car? the dispatcher says.

A grey one, I say.

And can you tell me, she says. Are they Hispanic? Are they Mexican?

They're white.

I pace up and down. It's tiring. It's tiring to be on the phone with her. It's tiring to hear the violence outside, and I think of the history of violence and of U.S. bombs and the whole world while listening to the woman talk on the phone. That viciousness is far, and this viciousness is near and pathetic.

I walk outside and see the woman. Her face is red. Makes her older. She's in her twenties—I know because I've seen her before—but she looks like she's carrying forty years. The man runs up to an apartment. I can't see him. He's a shadow. She follows with the baby.

•

There's a giant, white, Styrofoam cup shattered on the ground, and soda splashed and running into the asphalt—like blood—and the screaming on the street has died out.

•

I don't remember walking onto the parking lot, but I'm here, and the group is still looking at the now-empty space where the fighting had been. There's a guy on the phone with the police.

He knows more than me—watched them walk into the apartment. He knows where the violence is continuing.

As I walk by the group I hear, Mr. Martinez!

There's a student here, and I can't comprehend it because this is not a student's place. Their place is in the classroom on the far side of town.

When I turn, there's John surrounded by a small swarm of his friends, the most disruptive, funniest seventh-grader I taught last year. One who came from the reservation. One of the most problematic. One of the most hurt—with a sometimes abusive, sometimes apathetic mother, and a father he once told me he'd like to kill. One of my favorite kids.

But John isn't supposed to be here. John is from a different life, from over a year ago. John should be a dream.

Oh shit! I say, and I know it's not the best greeting for an old teacher to give a thirteen-year-old, but it's what comes out. What was all this? I say, thumbing toward the grey car and the poor remains of a struggle, because I don't know what to say or what to think or how to feel.

Some bitch about to get beat, he says.

He wants a response, and I want to tell him not to say that. I want to tell him not to talk about people like that, not to be sexist and mean. But he articulates it like he's proud. Because he told me once that I'm one of his favorite teachers, one of the best he'd ever had, probably ever would have, because he was going to drop out as soon as he could, because he wanted to shock me. He wants to prove that he's bad, that he's lost. I don't say anything, because he wants me to, because he knows I don't approve, because I know I don't have to.

You're still working over at the school, huh?

Yeah, I say. But I teach college now, too.

He needs to know this information because sometimes people get to do what they want to do. He needs to know sometimes lives can work out all right, for a while. He needs to know that it doesn't have to be like the lives of the students at school, where too many families are terrified of deportation and live in fear. The school whose kids have parents who threaten them not to talk about their abuse. The school that is in constant threat of losing its funding.

The cops show up.

One of the kids says, Hey, aren't we going to my house? My mom's not home.

We got to go smoke, Mr. Martinez, John says to me, and offers his hand. He doesn't fist bump. He shakes my hand, then floats away into the swarm, moving toward the houses behind my apartment complex.

One of the neighbors, the guy who was on the phone with the cops, comes over to me and keeps talking about how he was just walking outside to go get a haircut when he saw the fight. Seemed pretty excited about it.

I had to get my brother and get out here, he says. My brother and I do mixed martial arts.

Right, I say, and wonder if this is a guy who scares people back inside apartments, a guy who doesn't know what to do with feral people, or a guy who does what he's supposed to, who acts right.

His brother is nowhere to be found.

Who was that kid you were talking to? he says.

I don't know why he cares.

He was my student last year, I say, pointing to the direction John and his friends went.

Yeah? he says. I'm studying to be a probation officer. He'd better watch out. He was saying some pretty nasty stuff over there. I'd like to show him and his buddies that being hooligans doesn't pay. I'd straighten them out in a minute.

The neighbor points up at the cops banging on the couple's door.

That's what happens when you do drugs, he says.

His eyes aren't level, like his skull is crooked.

Some chain-smoking woman with her stomach spilling from her tank top comes over and starts chatting with another neighbor. The crooked-faced neighbor takes off to get that haircut, and I see John again, close to another building.

•

John, I yell out. I don't want him to go yet. I need to find words of wisdom. I have no words. But when I called him he stopped. Is this power? Is this responsibility?

So, I say. You live around here, then?

27

No, he says. I live down 75th.

John has the same bowl cut he had last year, crooked and cut badly in the same places. He looks the same. Still carries himself like he's not part of his swarm, like he's cooler, seen more shit, the way he did last year.

How's things been for you, man? I say.

All right, he says. How's everyone at the school?

All right, I say. You should watch out for those guys out there.

Shit, he says. They got to watch out for me.

Look, I want to say. Don't be screwing around. You know you're going to get yourself in trouble. I want to say something like that, but that's not right.

Instead, I ask if he remembers that part he played in *The Glass Menagerie* last year in class. I had all the kids switch up for different scenes. He asked to play two scenes as Amanda. Thought it was funny.

Yeah, he says, and laughs. I remember everything from your class, and all them stories you made us read, and how you didn't care when we cussed. That's why we like you, Mr. Martinez. You're not fake like the others. You don't front.

He smiles wide, but this is not a joke and this is not what I want to talk about. This isn't what I want to say.

Listen, I told you my brother's in prison because of dope, right? I say.

I want to talk about the miracle of being alone and sober in an apartment, writing a book instead of on the hunt. But I don't know how to say it.

Yeah. You told us. But *my* brother? he says and attempts to grin— as if he's trying to act like he's in a movie. My brother was killed because of shit *I* did, he says—says it like it's nothing. And since you last seen me I been to prison, Mr. Martinez, he says. For robbery.

And I'm probably going to go back, too. I'll probably fail my drug test.

Why? I say. What's the point?

I don't care, he says. Makes no difference.

What, I say. You like being locked up? You think juvey is fun?

Doesn't matter, he says. In there. Out here. I got people inside. It don't matter. I got shot since I last seen you, too.

You ain't got shot, I say. Bullshit.

He might be lying. But it might all be true. At least he's talking like it's true.

I did, he says. I swear. Swear on my life. I did. I got shot. In the shoulder.

Okay, I say. Didn't ask him to show me. He needs me to believe him. Whether it's true or not, he needs it to be true, and he's looking at me with those eyes. He wants to believe he has no faith in anything, because to think otherwise would crush him. There's nothing else to be done. Nothing I can think of.

He used to call me Dad last year. Thought it was hysterical. I thought it was weird, and told him to stop.

I don't think to give him my number, don't point to my apartment and say something like, Anytime you need, don't hesitate to come by. I don't do anything like that.

I say, John, don't do anything stupid.

You know me, Mr. Martinez, he says.

I know, I say. Don't do anything stupid.

Before he leaves I say, You were always one of my favorites.

I still am, he says, and smiles. He disappears with his swarm down the streets where I always get lost because all the houses look the same. The woman screams—muted—in the apartment above, and the cops are hammering on the door.

•

I have to leave to pick up my wife, and on the way home we drive toward the setting sun that catches fire in the desert—the great and terrible monster of the West—and it's fine. We give ourselves to it, and all we can do is watch.

David Martinez has an MFA in Creative Writing from the University of Riverside Low Residency program in Palm Desert. He has dual citizenship between the United States and Brazil, and has lived in Puerto Rico and all over the United States. David has conducted interviews for *The Coachella Review*, and his fiction has been published in *Broken Pencil*. When he is not teaching at Glendale Community College in Arizona he substitutes in elementary and middle schools. David is currently working on his first novel.

This story was previously published online by *Writers Resist*.

The Freedom of
Mothers Must Come

By Mbizo Chirasha

Pain scribbled signatures in these mothers' buttocks,
War tied ropes of struggle around these mothers' necks.
Songs of suffering are sung and unheard
in the congregations of townships and mountains
searching for freedoms' seeds.
The seeds of these mothers' wombs yearn for a freedom
too far away to be harvested, but not forgotten.

These mothers' bodies speak of truth.
These mothers' bodies carry scars.
These mothers' dimples are resilient,
These mothers' smiles and laughter offer hope.
These mothers' thighs are graffitied with bullet bruises,
the valleys of their backs reek
with the blood of their sons,
sons long buried in barrels of violence
their lives stolen in their greenness.

These mothers' hands trust the red clay soil,
even during cloudless seasons.
These mothers' wombs give birth to rays of dawn.
These mothers scribble memories on prison walls with rainbows
These mothers' shoulders carry the weight of journeys
and hope, which rises ripens dies
and rises again with each new day.

Mothers, how many times can you cough up sorrow?
For how many seasons can you sneeze with hunger?
You have eaten enough poverty
and licked the rough hand of a war long unforgotten
for too many dawns.

These mothers unburden propaganda from their shoulders
delete the baggage of political slogans from their breasts
abort the luggage of war from their wombs
These mothers turn to the hope of reaching pastures
where they can reap the fruits of freedom.

Mbizo Chirasha is an internationally acclaimed performance poet and writer, a creative and literary projects specialist, and an advocate of Girl Child Voices and Literacy Development. He is widely published in journals, magazines, and anthologies around the world. He co-edited *Silent Voices Tribute to Achebe Poetry Anthology*, Nigeria, and the *Breaking Silence Poetry* anthology, Ghana. His poetry collections include *Good Morning President*, Diaspora Publishers, 2011, and *United Kingdom and Whispering Woes of Ganges and*

Zambezi, Cyberwit Press, India, 2010. Visit his website at mbizotheblackpoet.wordpress.com.

This poem was previously published online by *Writers Resist.*

Going to Ground

By Sarah Einstein

Like a good citizen, I call my senators at least once a week these days, but their aides are brusque. They tell me that Alexander and Corker support the president's education agenda/healthcare reform/immigration order or whatever I'm outraged about on a given day. In the first few weeks, they'd thank me for my call. Now they simply say, "Your objection is noted," and hang up as quickly as they can. Once, as if caught off guard, one said, "Are you sure you live in Tennessee?"

I carry my passport with me everywhere these days.

I've begun to sort that which is precious from that which is not. I make a small pile of the things I'd pack in the night, a larger one of the stuff I would leave. Everyone is insisting we're just one Reichstag fire away from fascism. On the news, I watch a steady stream of black people murdered by the State for their blackness, and I think it's more likely that we've already had the Anschluss.

When I travel, I wear an inherited diamond I feel silly wearing at home. I remember being told when I was younger that a Jewish woman should always have enough jewelry on her body to bribe her way over a border. At the time it seemed quaint. Now it seems key. For the moment, the diamond ring's still on my finger. I wonder if there will come a day I'll need to sew it into the hem of my coat.

Over coffee, my friend Meredith talks about joining the resistance in a way that suggests we're headed for a war she thinks we can win. I talk about going to ground, about building false walls to hide people waiting for fake passports and safe transport. We scare ourselves and then laugh at ourselves, but after the laughing we are still scared.

Meredith wasn't always Meredith, and there is a passel of bills in our state legislature designed to make it impossible for her to be Meredith now. I tell her I will hide her in my hidden rooms, if it comes to that. She says she won't be hidden, but she might move to Atlanta.

My coffee these days is chamomile tea. I'm jittery enough as it is.

If we flee, we will go to my husband's family in Austria. They assure us that we'll be safe there, should it come to that, and I believe them. They've clearly learned lessons that we have not. The irony of this is not lost on me; there are Nazis in the family albums.

My husband has stopped talking about becoming an American citizen and started talking about being an anchor relative.

My friend Jessica is spending all her vacation time in Israel this year, establishing the Right of Return. I've stopped questioning the politics of this; refugees go where they can.

This Hanukah, I will give my niece and nephews passports if they don't already have them. If they do, I will give them whatever they ask for. I've lifted my moratorium on war toys. Maybe they should know how to handle a gun.

My closest disabled friends and I swap lists of medications and start to horde the things one or some of us need against the day we lose access to them. We read up on actual expiration versus labeled expiration dates. We refill prescriptions before we need to, just in case.

I have six boxes of Plan B in my closet, even though I'm long past childbearing years. On campus, I spread rumors about a shadowy network of old women who will help younger women with travel and money for abortions if they can't get the healthcare they need in their hometowns. I call all my old woman friends and build the network. I keep their names and numbers in handwritten lists and hide them away.

I refuse to let my husband put a "Stop Trump" bumper sticker on our car. "That's just foolish," I say. I let him keep the Cthulu fish. For now.

A young woman cries in my office, afraid that if she comes out to her parents they will disown her; she's still financially dependent on them. I tell her that she doesn't have to come out to them now, or ever, if she doesn't feel safe doing so. She looks shocked. It breaks my heart to have been the first to suggest the safety of the closet to her; I wonder what she is coming out of, if it had never occurred to her to remain in.

I've stopped going to protests and started going to meetings for which there are no flyers or Facebook event notices. To find them, you have to know someone who already has. We talk there of things I won't write here. At first, we turned off our phones. Now, we leave them at home.

And yet, still, like a good citizen, I call my senators at least once a week. Their aides are brusque. In the first few weeks, they'd thank me for my call. Now they hang up as quickly as they can. I haven't yet given up on the dream of America, but I'm making contingency plans.

Sarah Einstein teaches Creative Writing at the University of Tennessee at Chattanooga. Her essays and short stories have appeared in *The Sun*,

Ninth Letter, Still, and other journals, and been awarded a Pushcart and a Best of the Net. She is the author of *Mot: A Memoir* (University of Georgia Press, 2015) and *Remnants of Passion* (Shebooks, 2014). Visit Sara's website at www.saraheinstein.com.

This essay was previously published online by *Full Grown People* and *Writers Resist.*

Just a Short Note to Say Something You Already Know

By Lawrence Matsuda

For Donald's Daughter, Ivanka Trump

Ivanka, in a different time and place,
you and your children are squeezed into
cattle cars destined for Nazi death camps.
Stars pinned to your coats
and numbers tattooed on your arms.
Religion is your crime, something like
the 120,000 Japanese Americans whose race
incarcerates them during World War II.

If you dodge head shaving,
and starvation, maybe a country
would welcome you.

Angel of death is difficult to slip,
unfortunates are turned away,
chased by verbal brickbats and pitchforks.
You smell freedom's scent
but only glimpse porthole views
of Lady Liberty's tantalizing torch.

Doors slam and hands
of kindness withdraw.
You are not among privileged
huddled masses.

Today, as a 1% American demographic,
you are safe by an accident of birth.
Others less fortunate, however,
stand on precipices knowing,
"History does not repeat
itself but it rhymes."*

When Donald promises
a magnificent Great Wall
and spews religious
hatred to cheering crowds,
you must feel a guilty twinge,
knowing if this were 1943 Germany,
a chorus of incendiary voices
would echo and push innocents
off slippery cliffs into eternal darkness.
Black hole so forbidding victims
would never see their children again,
while self-serving politicians levitate

on bandwagons swerving on and off
a broken highway of eight million bones.

Lawrence Matsuda was born in the Minidoka War Relocation Center, a concentration camp for Japanese and Japanese Americans during WWII. He is a regional Emmy Award-winning writer and an author of two books of poetry, *A Cold Wind from Idaho* and *Glimpses of a Forever Foreigner*. Recently, he and Tess Gallagher collaborated on a book of poetry entitled *Boogie-Woogie Crisscross*, and chapter one of his graphic novel, *Fighting for America: Nisei Soldiers*, was animated and won a 2016 regional Emmy.

This poem was previously published in *Raven Chronicles* and *Writers Resist* online.

* Quote attributed to Mark Twain.

Vandals Desecrate Jewish Cemetery

By Laura Budofsky Wisniewski

Not that it's such a fancy graveyard,
just a hill, a mess,
stones leaning on each other
like the fathers of the bride and groom
after the wedding.
Our names are almost gone,
covered by a weeping moss.
I begged my son before I went, just burn me.
Do they listen?
Under all this dirt, tattooed numbers glow
like fireflies.
My Yacob used to say:
They're never done with us.
And I would think, so dark an eye
in such a handsome man?
Now his headstone's cracked like an egg.
Desecration?
Let's face it.
Small animals and even bears

have squatted on our sacred ruins.
That's not what drags my bones
here, as if fear were a wolf's tooth.
No, it's that I let myself believe
the world was getting better.

Laura Budofsky Wisniewski writes and teaches yoga in a small town in Vermont. Her work has appeared or is forthcoming in *Calyx, Minerva Rising, Hunger Mountain, Pilgrimage* and other journals. Her grandparents were immigrants fleeing persecution.

This poem was previously published online by *Writers Resist.*

Cagey

By Koushik Banerjea

"What are you doing?"

He was surprised by the question, believing himself to have been alone. He had been admiring himself in a shard of mirror he had found, discarded on the dirt road snaking around the park. Gauging his reflection, he tried to look haughty, then severe, by turns flaring his nostrils then dulling his eyes. Was it obvious he was a thief? He didn't think so, not any more.

"You! I asked you a question. Are you deaf?"

He turned around hoping the disdain didn't show. His questioner stood, feet apart, in the familiar khaki uniform of the police. The man was carrying a *bhuri*, a little Ganesh potbelly, sagging over his belt, and in that one detail could be spied so much of what would always divide them. As much as the uniform or the steel tipped *lathi*, it was the softness of that belly, its partiality to sweetmeats and greed, which marked out this man's tribe.

"No, sir. I was just leaving, sir," he said to the policeman, observing the expected protocol but knowing from the deep-set rituals of the cage that it meant nothing.

He watched as the policeman prodded a bundle of rags a little further along the path. The rags began to stir and a disheveled face appeared, already terrorized long before the steel tip brushed its chin. He realized then his good fortune in even being afforded the courtesy of a question. Standing there with a shard of glass in one hand, he could just as easily have been deemed a threat by the policeman. The city was on edge, the bodies still fresh, and he was taking a risk each time he drifted away from the huddle. He knew he had to hurry back to his brothers, still prone on the same benches where they'd eventually found one another, to warn them of the danger. But when he did, he saw to his relief that they were already awake, sitting up for the policeman's benefit like a couple of early morning *bhadralok*, discussing current affairs. The lathi briefly paused, satisfying itself that these were indeed gentlemen and not miscreants, before moving on to the next set of unfortunates.

And watching this, with the shard now safely wrapped in a fold of his vest, it made him think how no one ever asked the right questions. It had been just the same when he was in the cage.

•

Picking away at the scab, he felt a certain amount of regret. Space was limited here and he had taken to marking his tiny locale with whatever was at hand. More often than not this involved hair (his own), or a chipped fingernail, and on one occasion a tooth unhooked by day after day of the cage gruel. But today he had noticed a scab building up on his forearm, and the urge to scratch the itch had proven too great to resist. The skin had not yet flaked, so his action drew blood and pus. He didn't mind too much, though, as it made for a richer signature on the floor. He knew the other inmates would be looking at him as he pinched the skin, then released the gunk; knew as well that there would be no complaints, the memory still fresh of those other days when it was *their* teeth or blood that had lined the floor.

He sensed that his blood had been in some way corrupted by the surroundings. Now even the mosquitoes tended to avoid him on their nighttime sorties. The moan and slap of the other wretches meant they were still being plagued by malarial torments, yet *his* nights were oddly peaceful. He would hold the gruel down and continue to build himself up with press-ups on his knuckles. And he would watch, and wait. The wretches would occasionally come to blows with one another, but even when this happened they were careful not to allow their dispute to spill over into the micro-fiefdom he had marked out for himself. His vest started to fill out with this taut system rigour, vein and fibre and barely concealed violence in those arms; the knuckles long since cured of the taste of floor, safeguarded as they were by an extra layering of skin. And though he was young, one of the youngest in fact in the cage, there was now a strong beard shielding that face.

And then one day the news he had been so desperate to hear. News he had waited so long for that there *were* times when his resolve had nearly crumbled, when he had imagined that this was what his life would always be. Yet when it finally came it was delivered without ceremony. A perfunctory 'You!' and the unlocking of bolts. Space, which he now knew to be the most precious of companions, was apparently needed for another kind of inmate, and with a final reminder that he was a lucky *badmaash* ringing in his ears, the system spat the thief back out into the dust and the tumult.

•

No one was there to meet him, and after the initial disappointment, which was barely even that, he felt nothing. Shielding his eyes from the harsh glare of late morning, he squinted at the first building that lay beyond the dirt track and at the thick plume of smoke that was rising from it.

•

"Bhaiyya," implored a man, skeletal arms thrust outwards, that simple action evidently so draining that no more words would come.

He paused to look at the man, noting the distant saucers of eyes set back in hollow sockets. Instinctively he reached up to soothe the bridge of his own nose with thumb and forefinger; felt surprised when the fingers traced thick hair in the space just below his cheekbones; strode on purposefully towards the plume without looking back.

•

As he crossed the waste ground, his eyes picked out more stricken figures, little more than shapes really, only the occasional spasm indicating any life at all. Mostly, they were just covered in rags, though one or two were still sitting, as though meditating, in the clothes they must have been wearing when their lives were touched by fire or tragedy or whatever it was that had left them like this.

He could hardly bring himself to look at these figures, so implacable did they appear in their sadness. It was even worse with the ones who called out to him, begging for food or, perhaps, just comfort.

"Dada. Bhaiyya. Amar ke kichu ekta ditte parben?"

"Dada. Amar khidda."

Or sometimes, just "Dada." *Dada*, though he was barely old enough to be considered anyone's Dada. He looked at their arms, little more than flesh starved twigs really, and felt something surging up within him. At this stage, there was still no sign of his own brothers, whose Dada he actually was by virtue of being the eldest. Even so, he found himself studying the blank faces on display for any traces of recognition. Perhaps his brothers no longer looked the same?

He had heard how beards were grown or heads sometimes shaved. He knew people had done what they could, had often had no choice but to hide in plain sight. There had been whispers in the cage, the most recent arrivals breathing terrible tales of riot and flame, cleaver and bone. And he had absorbed it all, shape-shifting imperceptibly from a thief to a warrior.

People change, he thought, even in a short space of time. He had seen that for himself in the cage. Right in front of him, big, strong men reduced to urchins, the fight drawn out of their faces with one savage beating. The unexpectedness of it, perhaps the shame, but either way all that swagger absorbed by the blows, repainted as something smaller, delivered in silence.

Yet these figures around him now were of complete strangers, and in that sense should have exerted no more pull on his imagination than the boundary markers of detritus in the cage. So when he looked again, this time more closely, and saw that they were in fact not meditating but sitting on recently bandaged stumps, he was as surprised as anyone that the thing surging through him, up through his gut and into his throat, then out of his head, felt more primal than anything he had experienced behind bars.

Koushik Banerjea is a London-based writer. His work is featured in *Verbal* magazine and *darkmatter: in the ruins of imperial culture*. "Cagey" is set in the turbulent period leading up to the Partition of India, in 1947. The timing feels apt this year, which marks the 71st anniversary of those traumatic events, but also the inauguration of deep disquiet at political upheavals on both sides of the Atlantic. This story was previously published online by *Writers Resist*.

Sighting Posts

By D.A. Gray

Last time I visited the country of fear an old friend greeted me at its capital.

In another life we would meet for beers at the VFW. Neither talked much.

Before tonight, when my friend suddenly remembered the first rifle his daddy put in his hands. He cocks his red cap back, wipes his forehead with a napkin,

stares for a minute as if spreading out the pieces of the story on the bar counter before assembling them. The he begins. "We stood in the pasture. Daddy put

the butt against my shoulder, pushed it in hard, and said for me to put my cheek against the wood. 'You see the can on the fencepost?' 'Yep.' A red, white

and blue Budweiser can still full. 'Now see it over the sighting post. When you got the target, squeeze the trigger.' I could never close my other eye back then. He got tired of waiting and said 'Take your time.' I knew he was tired because he repeated 'Take your time.' The third time he said, 'Think of the kid that knocked you off the seesaw at school.' I pulled, and the barrel pulled right and the can stayed on

the post. I lifted my head and scanned for some patch of dust
in the twenty acres of pasture. He said nothing. Just walked over to
the post, grabbed the can and chugged it, then chugged the other can
he'd been holding.

I couldn't focus on it back then.

Now I see sighting posts everywhere."

D.A. Gray's poetry collection, *Contested Terrain*, was recently released by FutureCycle Press. His previous collection, *Overwatch*, was published by Grey Sparrow Press, 2011. His work has appeared in *The Sewanee Review, Appalachian Heritage, The Good Men Project, Writers Resist, Rise Up Review*, and *War, Literature and the Arts*, among many other journals. Gray holds an MFA from The Sewanee School of Letters and an MS from Texas A&M–Central Texas. A retired soldier and veteran, the author writes and lives in Central Texas.

Patriarchy

patriarchy: a system in which men hold power, to which women's access is systematically restricted, and within which women can expect harassment and denigration—yet they persist

patriarch: one of those guys mentioned above

Smashing, on the preceding page, is by Kit-Bacon Gressitt, a haphazard photographer and the publisher and a founding editor of *Writers Resist*.

The Woman Candidate

By Caralyn Davis

"You crave power," they said.

"Everyone who runs for president craves power. You need power to get things done," the woman candidate said. "The question is: What will each of us do with that power?"

"Women shouldn't want that much power. You're corrupt," they said. "Look, here's an article from a website our friends like that proves you're corrupt. You're a sleazy thief, an unpatriotic traitor, a murderer, a child molester, a slave owner. You're also probably dying of a dread disease. You're any caricature we can think of that justifies the fact that our skin crawls because you are powerful—and you seek more power still."

"I want to help you, but I won't make promises that aren't attainable in the here and now," the woman candidate said.

"You're evil," they said.

"I never claimed to be perfect, but I always did my best for the American people. Could you listen to what I have to say—consider my policy proposals?" the woman candidate said.

"You're evil," they said.

"Is it just me? Would you listen to another woman who doesn't supplicate men?" the woman candidate said.

"Of course," they said.

"Here's my daughter. She has two master's degrees and a doctorate," the woman candidate said.

"She's evil too, and that's nepotism—she's never worked a day in her life," they said.

"Here's the woman minority leader of the U.S. House of Representatives. She helped millions more Americans get healthcare at great political cost, and she helped pass an interim federal budget that keeps funding key programs when the president and his party wanted them cut," the woman candidate said.

"She's Hollywood liberal elite, trying to gut the values of the heartland, or she's a neoliberal corporate shill. We can't make up our minds, but either way, we hate her," they said.

"Here's a woman senator, a former state attorney general," the woman candidate said.

"With those tits and that ass, she slept her way into every job she's had," they said.

"Here's a woman senator who worked as a waitress to help pay her way through law school," the woman candidate said.

"Talking the way she does, she's unbalanced—hysterical," they said.

"Here's a fourteen-term congresswoman who champions the working class, women, and people of color," the woman candidate said.

"She's a racist conspiracy theorist, plus her wigs are as manly as your pantsuits," they said.

"Here's …" the woman candidate said.

"Not her either," they said.

Caralyn Davis lives in Asheville, North Carolina, and works as a freelance writer/editor for trade publications in the healthcare and technology transfer fields. Her fiction and creative nonfiction have appeared in *Word Riot, Eclectica, Flash Fiction Magazine, The Doctor T.J. Eckleburg Review, Superstition Review, EXPOUND, Monkeybicycle,* and other journals. She likes cat acrobatics, and she can be found on Twitter @CaralynDavis.

This piece was previously published online by *Writers Resist.*

Winning Campaign

By Karthik Purushothaman

I wear 140 characters
as pinstripes and say
what I think

without thinking.
My superpower is fitting
both feet in my mouth

and projectile vomiting
the stuff between my toes.
I save the reporters

from jumping off buildings,
leaping across canyon
-deep cracks and swimming

upstream to the source
where the current is strongest
and I am the current

world record holder
for the tallest bungee-jump
into a smoldering hot

Geisha, doing three and a half
twirls on the way down
3D-printing

Escher knots
with my throw-up,
bringing samurai swords

to gunfights, and writing
the book of moonlight
so vote for me.

Karthik Purushothaman comes from Chennai, India. Since earning his MFA at William Paterson University, he has been teaching undergraduates there and at New Jersey City University. He is currently putting together his first collection of poems entitled *Legal Alien*, as a tribute to his U.S. Department of Homeland Security-assigned status (also the refrain of a Sting/Shinehead song). His poetry has appeared in *Rattle, The Common, The Margins, The Puritan, Writers Resist, EVENT*, and elsewhere. Grateful to be a part of this inaugural anthology of resistance, Karthik has also been nominated for a 2017 Pushcart Prizes and the Best New Poets 2018 anthologies.

This poem was previously published online by *Writers Resist.*

Clarion Reminder

By Laura Grace Weldon

The powerful provoke the powerless
to push against one another.
Their power grows by keeping us
in all kinds of prisons.

Yet we are not powerless.

Remember the black bear
roaming Clarion County, Pennsylvania,
its head trapped a month or more
in a metal-ringed pail.

Remember those who chased it for hours,
grabbed it in a perilous embrace,
carefully sawed loose those tight bonds.
Imagine what they felt as the bear
ran free into the woods.
Imagine, too, the bear.

Laura Grace Weldon is the author of a poetry collection, *Tending,* and a handbook of alternative education, *Free Range Learning.* She has a collection of essays scheduled for release in 2019. Laura has written poetry with nursing home residents, used poetry to teach conflict resolution, and painted poems on beehives, although her work appears in more conventional places, such as *J Journal, Penman Review, Literary Mama, Christian Science Monitor, Mom Egg Review, Dressing Room Poetry Journal, Shot Glass Journal,* and others. Connect with her website, lauragraceweldon.com, or on Twitter @earnestdrollery.

This poem was previously published online by *Writers Resist.*

The Tao that Trump Won't Hear

By H.L.M. Lee

When I take my younger daughter to school, I see the rush of her first grade friends running to hug each other and share head lice (much to the chagrin of every parent). My daughter's BFF has a father from England and a mother from Maine. Another girl's father is Muslim and her mother is— I don't know. My own two daughters are Chinese-Italian. They have friends who are African-American and Hispanic. One neighborhood boy has a blended family with a mother and two fathers. I am seldom overwhelmed by emotion, but the morning drop-off often makes me choke up. To these children, unconcerned about the larger world around them, all that matters is the joy in shouting about their newest toy or the treat they have for snack time.

Lately, when I sit alone in my office and stare at the computer screen, I find myself choking up for a different reason. I imagine the death of Martin Luther King, Jr.'s vision, that the arc of the moral universe bends toward justice. In my more cynical moods, I give up and accept a world where, for my girls and girls everywhere, their gender is an insurmountable obstacle to reaching their potential. The sadness strikes me like the loss of a friend and I fight tears, because a man who couldn't pass the vetting for babysitter has been elected president.

It takes a team of architects, carpenters, electricians, plumbers, decorators and more to build a house, but only one person with a match to burn it down. The Trump administration is making a shambles of democracy, damaging the environment, perverting our humanity and turning from knowledge. He has fired James Comey, Director of the FBI. Whatever you think of Comey, the action of firing the man investigating Trump and those around him should ring every fire alarm in the country.

In this dispiriting time, I have been reading the *Tao Te Ching* and keeping it on my nightstand. A classic Chinese text of 81 short chapters, it embodies a philosophy of *Tao* (pronounced "dow"), which has been described as *Path* or *Way*, referring to right conduct. This interpretation, however, is only a shadow of *Tao*'s many layers of meaning, which underlie all we are and all we perceive. The second word *Te* (pronounced "deh") is often translated as *Virtue*, but virtue from following the *Tao* rather than transitory social rules.

Attributed to Lao-Tzu, who may or may not have been an actual person, and originating about 2,500 years ago, the *Tao Te Ching* is the basis of Taoism, one of Asia's major religions, though it mentions no deity.

> The Tao that can be told is not the eternal Tao.
> The name that can be named is not the eternal name.
> —Chapter 1

Tao itself is undefinable—even in the original Chinese as these first lines admit. Yet, the *Tao Te Ching* with its terse poetry and insight resonates for many across enormous differences in time and culture. For me it is now a needed source of perspective.

Lifted from their metaphysical context, lines from the *Tao Te Ching* sound like the epigram in a fortune cookie, but Lao Tzu's advice to Chinese lords is as relevant in the age of Donald Trump as it was 2,500 years ago.

> Oversharpen the blade, and the edge will soon blunt.
> . . .
> Claim wealth and titles, and disaster will follow.
> —Chapter 9

Can there be a better summation of Trump's path? All his life he has crowed about his wealth and status. But creditors repossessed his 281-foot yacht in 1991 and imminent ruin forced him to take a $916 million write-off in 1995. He would have been richer investing his money in the S&P 500 and leaving it alone, instead of developing businesses and buildings. Trump Airlines was a bust. Trump University was a sham. Trump Steaks were greasy and tasteless.

> The way of nature is unchanging.
> Knowing constancy is insight.
> Not knowing constancy leads to disaster.
> —Chapter 16

"No drama" Obama's steadiness during eight years as president contrasts sharply with Trump's contradictory statements—*often in the same sentence.* Trump says that unpredictability gives him the advantage in business. Maybe, but it would be catastrophic in governance and we are seeing its harrowing consequences in real time.

Those who boast achieve nothing.
Those who brag will not endure.
—Chapter 24

Trump has the "best words." He called the Trump Taj Mahal casino the "Eighth Wonder of the World"—before it went bankrupt and cost him real estate, the yacht I have already mentioned, his private plane, and his helicopter. Can anyone trust a man who masqueraded as his own publicist to bray about affairs with celebrities? Unlike the "fine tuned machine" that Trump touted, his White House lurches like Boris Karloff's Frankenstein from one self-inflicted crisis to another.

Easy promises make for little trust.
Taking things lightly results in great difficulty.
—Chapter 63

Trump pandered to supporters by saying he could "make possible every dream you have ever dreamed." That's not a campaign promise, that's a skeevy pickup line. "We're going to have insurance for everybody … great healthcare," he vowed, "It will be in a much-simplified form. Much less expensive and much better." Now that Trumpcare has passed the House—promising, instead, to throw tens of millions off health insurance and eliminate protections for those with pre-existing conditions—will his supporters finally take off their beer goggles and see, by the cold light of morning, who they brought home?

Knowing ignorance is strength.
Ignoring knowledge is sickness.
—Chapter 71

Science begins by accepting ignorance then moves toward knowledge. That's how we learned to launch rockets into space and harness electricity, how we developed the Big Bang theory and quantum mechanics, and why we cook pork. To curtail the study of climate change, Trump seeks to cut funding for NOAA weather satellites, which would hobble the ability to forecast tornadoes and hurricanes, and endanger lives in the process.

> Why are the people starving?
> Because the rulers eat up the money in taxes.
> . . .
> Why are the people rebellious?
> Because the rulers interfere too much.
> —Chapter 75

Superficially, these lines support conservative beliefs that people are taxed too much and government regulations are a burden. But the brevity of the *Tao Te Ching* requires delving beneath the surface. Two chapters later is a more expansive passage:

> The Tao of heaven is to take from those who have too much and give
> to those who do not have enough.
> Ordinary people act differently.
> They take from those who do not have enough to give to those who
> already have too much.
> Who has more than enough and gives it to the world?
> Only the wise.
> —Chapter 77

If people starve, it is from taxation in the broader sense, from the wealthy taking too much as they fight the minimum wage and the social safety net, leaving the 99 percent to work more and more for less and less.

If people rebel, it is from interference with women's control of their bodies; interference with civil rights and the right to vote; interference with the right to live, love and worship freely. These were the cries from protesters on Boston Common the day after Trump's inauguration. My family and I were there, shouting with them, an official estimate of 175,000. But a number can't convey the visceral punch from seeing broad patches of pink, like flowers, spread across the Common. The patches were masses of pussy hats and each flower was a woman, man or child gathered on that brisk, sunny day. I stood in awe, seeing that crowd filling the grounds in common cause.

Now, every morning I wake at 5:30 and lie quietly, a mundane start but one that prepares me for the day. At breakfast, I listen to the news and steel myself against yet another assault on government and society. The list of what's at stake is overwhelming, but I find the will to persist in these words, implicitly reminding me that water can wear away stone—if it flows and agitates:

> Under heaven nothing is more soft and yielding than water.
> Yet for attacking the solid and strong, nothing is better;
> It has no equal.
>
> —Chapter 78

H.L.M. Lee is an electronics engineer with a background in English literature. While owning and operating a small high-tech company, he also writes web content and marketing materials, and develops video scripts for a peer reviewed scientific journal. He has recently finished a novel, *Bleeding in Babylon*, about the Iraq War. All passages from *Tao Te Ching* were translated by Gia-fu Feng and Jane English, with Toinette Lippe, Third Vintage Books edition, 2011.

This essay was previously published online by *Writers Resist*.

Letter from Guantanamo

By Laura Orem

Seasons don't matter except
for the discomfort they bring.
June is just hotter.

The Caribbean thuds against Cuba,
steaming like soup, saltier
than our tears,
if anyone cried here.

Whether we bear it or not,
the pain continues.

The interrogator takes his work
as seriously as Michelangelo
considered the perfect pink
of God's fingertips.

Once I ate sweet dates and dreamed
of doing something important.

Now the sun, that holy eye,
stares down on the sea and sand,
strikes us blind.

Laura Orem is the author of *Resurrection Biology* (Finishing Line Press 2017) and the chapbook *Castrata: a Conversation* (Finishing Line Press 2014), and she's a featured writer at the *Best American Poetry* blog. Laura received an MFA in Writing and Literature from Bennington College and taught writing for many years at Goucher College in Baltimore. Her poetry, essays and art have appeared in many journals, including *Nimrod, Zocalo Public Square, DMQ, Everlasting Verses, Blueline, Atticus Review, Barefoot Review, OCHO, and Mipoesias.* Laura is a poetry editor at *Writers Resist,* and she lives on a small farm in Red Lion, Pennsylvania with her husband, three dogs, and so many cats she's afraid to say.

This poem was previously published in *Resurrection Biology* and *Writers Resist* online.

Prayer

By IE Sommsin

God, will you forgive the sins of our times,
this sad era, its soft habits of thought
and the glib assumptions easily taught
that breed the lying slogans worse than crimes?
We cannot help how the words work to cloud
and clog and flood the forums of the mind.
They build the thick high walls that keep us blind
and kill the calm silence with all that's loud.
Myth, wild tales, and the clever fools come cheap,
and the boldly stupid prompt great cheering,
while the magical, repeated, jeering
accusation makes the shallow look deep.
You in the future will know what I feel
when your nation's caught on history's wheel.

IE Sommsin, a writer and artist from Kentucky, lives in San Francisco and has a fondness for sonnets.

This poem was previously published online by *Writers Resist.*

Fun to Be Fabulous

By C. Gregory Thompson

In December 2016, a month almost to the day after Donald J. Trump became our nation's 45th president-elect, we, the shell-shocked, were still trying to comprehend. All of us—every single person I knew, barring the occasional deluded Facebook friend I didn't know was so full of hate—were still reeling from the surrealistic reality of what had happened just weeks before. Of what hit us, a gut punch no one saw coming. A punch thrown so hard to the solar plexus as to knock the collective air out of us.

"You look just like my aunt," a woman said, looking at my friend, Sara. "But, of course, she's dead now."

Struck mute by this out of left-field comment, we weren't sure if it was part of the new hell we were trying to survive. It so very easily could have been.

We were perched on the aqua blue cushions of an outdoor couch on what we jokingly referred to as the "lanai" at Rancho Las Palmas, a high-end resort in Palm Desert, California. The lanai and this particular couch had become our regular spot for the past three-and-a-half years—from its catty-corner vantage point, we could see everyone coming and going. Graduates of the UCR-Palm Desert

Low-Residency MFA Creative Writing program, we'd returned to our alma mater's "residency" to visit our professors, fellow alumni, and current students.

The woman standing before us wasn't one of us. We'd never seen her before. We looked up at her, waiting.

"You see, I'm Robert Kardashian's sister," she continued.

Sara, always game for a little crazy, said, "So, you think I look Armenian?"

"There's no such thing as an Armenian; they're all Jews who haven't accepted Jesus," the woman—we never did learn her first name—replied without missing a beat. I still have no idea what that means. Long ago, I stopped trying to figure it out. With Trump, nonsensical, not-based-in-reality, untruthful speech had become the norm. Crazy was now a fact of our lives.

This exchange took place the first week of December. The desert winter weather was mild enough to sit outside. A calm sweetness hung in the air, an atmosphere usual to Palm Springs and the reason people liked to visit. You could almost believe the poisoned air the rest of the country breathed couldn't get through. You could almost pretend that what had happened never had. Almost. Being in Palm Springs provided a temporary balm from the new societal dis-ease caused by the rise of Make America Great Again. And the crazy lady's antics took our minds off it even further, if temporarily so.

Earlier, I'd noticed the woman roaming the lanai, stopping to chat with people who walked through the area or were seated at other couches and chairs. Mid-sixties to early-seventies, smartly-dressed in a designer-ish pantsuit and gold jewelry, hair highlighted to a bronze color, about five foot six, she looked like the average well-to-do Palm Springs visitor or resident and carried an oversized red tote bag with gold lettering.

The woman had placed the bag on the edge of the stone fire pit we sat around like it was part of her armor. The way the bag scrunched down, I couldn't read the lettering or see what it portended, but after the Jesus comment, my crazy-antennas were in full salute, gyrating back and forth. A bit like slowing down to look at a car accident—you want to, but you don't want to, fearful of what you might see, but still curious—we watched to see how far the crazy might go.

"Kris is a horrible person," she said. "She ruined the family as soon as she married into it. And she poisoned my brother. They called it esophageal cancer, but it was a poisoning."

Sara and I threw sidelong glances at each other, asking with our eyes, is she for real? She definitely had our attention. In the whacked-out world of the Kardashians, maybe Kris did poison Robert. Isn't anything possible—especially now? Fake news everywhere. The Kardashian name still floating about. That poisoned air hovering right at the edge of the Coachella Valley pushed harder to gain access. Trump's tiny hands clawing over the San Jacinto Mountains waved down at us.

"Then, when she married that freak, she destroyed the family."

Her verbs gradually took on more power. First "ruined" now "destroyed." *Freak* implied Caitlyn, we assumed. I wondered, did Caitlyn become a freak to this woman after the Bruce to Caitlyn transition, or was that a moniker she'd always used for Bruce? Listening to her, and, admittedly, not being a fan of Kris, Caitlyn, or the whole Kardashian mess, it was fun to hear her trash the family. I didn't have to look at Sara to know that she was enjoying this teardown, even if false, as much as I was. The fact that Caitlyn was a Republican, a Trump supporter, *and* transgender made this whole fucked-up stew reek of total annihilation and utter weirdness.

"Thank God Kourtney has a brain, and Khloé has a heart, because Kim has a hole in her soul."

Eloquently said, I thought. Sadly, Kim's soul hole was fast-spreading to so many others in this country. In part, a result of her family's own fakeness, uber-materialism, and celebrity-level self-promotion. Did they sound like anyone else? Maybe like that inhuman, orange-haired freak now pretending in the Oval Office.

Before she picked up her red bag, the woman left us with these words: "It's all okay as long as we accept God."

Her parting comment made perfect sense in the context of her insanity. Because, belief in God made every horrible act, every comment or posting full of hate towards someone not like yourself, every hollow, empty-souled person's existence, allowable, okay and reasonable.

After she was gone, I looked at Sara and said, "I highly doubt she's his sister or a Kardashian."

Sara ran inside to ask the front desk. A few moments later, she returned.

"The concierge said, 'She isn't a Kardashian, but it's fun to be fabulous.' Did you notice her bag?" Sara asked.

I knew it was bright red and large, big enough to carry a lot of stuff, but beyond that nothing stuck out.

"Trump. Trump International Hotel Las Vegas."

That was the lettering I hadn't been able to read. And it was the perfect coda to our interaction with the crazy woman. I hoped the bag wasn't leather. I hoped it was pleather or just pimped out plastic, because that would be apt for the over-saturated red color and gleaming gold lettering. I hoped it was as fake as all that it stood for now that the man with that name was the so-called president.

Carrying her bag around didn't necessarily mean she was a Trump supporter. Maybe she'd picked it up before he became our president-elect, but it did sow a little doubt and raised the whole experience up a level. Sara, who had seen the Trump lettering on the bag, told me she'd assumed the woman was a Trump supporter, and knowing that had tainted the whole experience for her. She was cool with the woman being crazy and impersonating a Kardashian, but as a Trump supporter too, it gave Sara the serious willies.

Somehow it made sense that she was team Make America Great Again. She could easily be the type not to see through the veneer, to be drawn into the glitz, the flash, the money, and the fake everything—overlooking common decency, human rights, and national security. After all, she had a fascination with the Kardashians.

While Sara and I did giggle and gossip about her and wonder who she really was, the whole experience was actually sad. Later, I spotted her being seated for lunch on the outdoor dining terrace. She'd changed clothes and still looked quite put-together, but after spending the last several hours wandering the resort, trying to impress strangers, she ate alone. Sad too, she'd decided to co-opt the Kardashian name. To make herself feel more important, out of boredom and loneliness, or was it sheer madness? Trying to understand, it all became too tied up in what was happening in our own country. The similarities to President Cheeto Head, from all we'd heard and knew about the man, didn't escape me. Like Kim, he had a burning hole in his soul. And, like this woman, he was probably horribly lonely and unhappy, despite the swirl of sycophantic madness around him.

Reality TV, in part, gave us the so-called president. It moved the dial further in the direction of crazy and provided a platform for Trump and his cronies. This woman was part of that; she was affected by what she saw happening with the Kardashians enough to make herself one of them. To top it off, she carried a big red bag with Trump's name emblazoned across it. A double-whammy of reality world unreality. The problem for the rest of us? Their fake reality had become our frightening authentic reality.

Fifteen months after meeting the fake Kardashian, he'd been president long enough to call this period of time the Trump era. From his first day in office, he'd wreaked havoc, and we still couldn't catch our breath. Each day was a new fiasco, insult or horror, and nothing had really changed now that he'd been in office for a while. Writing this, I questioned my own compassion—a thing I would have liked to see more of coming from the Republicans, the conservatives. If she was truly mentally ill, shouldn't I have had compassion for her? What about him? His behavior seemed like that of an unbalanced person. Should I have compassion for him too?

In both cases, I probably could, somewhere within my own belief system, although it pained me to admit that when it came to him. However, the part of me living through this hell he and his so-called party created didn't have any compassion at all. I saw her, and people like her, as part of the problem. A problem without a solution. And maybe that was wrong of me, but I thought it was that confounding to most of us. How to reconcile the people we were and truly wanted to be in the face of a monster like him?

Our conversation with the woman was a small moment, a blip in time. But somehow it was huge too. Because, to me, to us, Sara and me, it said so much. This woman did not want to be who she really and truly was. She wanted to be someone else. Her life was not enough. She wanted bigger and better, a name of the moment—Kardashian. To be *that* fabulous.

Back then, after she left, we continued to sit on the lanai watching the world move around us. The air returned to its Palm Springs winter sweetness, and a calm quietude descended. We could go back to momentarily pretending that the world hadn't ended on November 8, 2016. And yet, that poisoned air at the edge of the desert, desperate to encroach, still hung too close; those tiny diseased hands that wanted to creep further down the mountains still made the hair on the back of my neck stand up. We couldn't make believe much longer.

Pretending that reality is not real ultimately won't work. Pretending that Trump is not the horrible human being he is, or believing his lifestyle has any basis in reality, will doom us all. And, for the woman on the lanai, pretending to be someone she is not will only lead to loneliness and misery, and, even, to that dreaded hole in her soul.

She might be there already.

C. Gregory Thompson, a Pushcart Prize nominee, lives in Los Angeles, California, where he writes fiction, nonfiction, plays, and memoir. His work has appeared or is forthcoming in *Storgy Magazine, Writers Resist, Five:2:One, Cowboy Jamboree, Full Grown People, The Offbeat, Printers Row Journal,* and *Reunion: The Dallas Review.* Four of his short stories were included in the 2017 New Short Fiction Series. He was named a finalist in the Tennessee Williams/New Orleans Literary Festival's 2015 Fiction Contest. His short play "Cherry" won two playwriting awards. He earned an MFA in Creative Writing and Writing for the Performing Arts at the University of California, Riverside/Palm Desert. He is the founder of Pen & Paper Writing Workshops. Follow him on Twitter @cgregthompson and Instagram @cgregorythompson.

This essay was previously published online by *Writers Resist.*

For the Duration: Ten Strategies

By Judy Viertel

1. Tell Joke

Lisa and Henry used to linger over the morning paper together, sipping cup after steaming cup of coffee. Now, Lisa can't stand to read any part of it except the movie reviews. As for Henry, he resents having to process the onslaught of bad news on his own.

He tries reading the news to her in a Donald Duck voice, hoping to amuse her. He tries changing the s's to 'x's: "The prexident has xaid he won't anxwer quextions regarding hix invextmentx."

"Invextmentx," Lisa says, her lips fixed in a straight line. It's hard for her to tell, now, what's supposed to be funny.

2. Seek Mediation

They sign up for counseling. After a few visits, Janice, the therapist, confronts Henry: "Lisa doesn't want to hear about the news. It's making her sick."

Lisa smiles. But then Janice turns on her. "As the son of Chinese immigrants, Henry feels a responsibility to stay informed about civil rights. You'll both need be more accommodating."

In her wiry, ergonomic chair, Janice's back suddenly slumps.

Later, Henry and Lisa discuss this: They wonder if Janice, too, is having trouble sleeping.

3. Take Breaks

As a concession to Henry, Lisa tries using Facebook to stay caught up on national events. After each political post she reads, she switches to the feed of an old school friend. This woman has a three-year-old, a five-year-old and two cats. She bakes. She posts images of all her little creatures nuzzling each other and snapshots of smeary rainbow cupcakes. Lisa burns with envy: Everything in the woman's life, it seems, is messy and ripe.

4. Make Lists

Janice suggests they enumerate the things they're grateful for.

Lisa writes, "old novels, strawberries, zumba class."

Henry writes, "independent news sources, Golden Gate Park, trips abroad, my mother's dandan noodles."

Lisa looks at his list and adds "trips" to hers.

Henry looks at hers and adds "strawberries."

In a few months, they promise each other, it will be spring.

5. Visualize

The president's voice makes Lisa nauseous. One night she turns to Henry, who's also still awake, and explains. "When I was working at the campus copy center, the manager kept bumping into me, allegedly 'on accident.' He had reddish skin and squinty eyes. I just realized: That's who the president reminds me of."

"He reminds me of this guy who worked at the video arcade near my high school. He kept asking where I was 'from.' Arlington, I'd say. 'No,' he'd say, 'you were made in Taiwan, weren't you?' Then he'd laugh."

The next day at her gym, Lisa watches TV with closed captions while she uses the treadmill. The president is giving a speech. Speeding up, she imagines herself trampling him under the rolling belt.

6. Cultivate Distraction

Lisa keeps buying ice cream.

"We can't just watch movies and eat dessert," Henry says.

"It's a new flavor," Lisa calls out from the kitchen. "Toasted hazelnut. And we meant to see this movie when it came out. Remember?"

"Okay, maybe in half an hour? I want to watch the news." Henry watches. Soon, he's muttering at the screen.

From the bedroom, Lisa calls out, "Just turn it off." She closes her eyes and breathes. She's attempting one of Janice's relaxation techniques.

Henry leaves the TV on, but stops muttering. Instead, he cuts a sliver from a post-it note, coloring it black. He sticks it on the screen. He whispers, "Want to be Hitler? There's your mustache, dude."

7. Substitute

Henry flies east to see his mother, who's been ill. He sleeps in his old bed. On the ceiling, there's a dog-shaped water stain he remembers from childhood.

In the morning his mother tries making oatmeal, but forgets to turn on the burner. "I'm fine," she insists.

Henry spends the day calling eldercare facilities. In the evening, the two of them watch the news.

"What happened to that nice black man?" Henry's mother asks. "Every time I turn on the TV, I see that comic actor from long ago. Ugly man."

Later, Henry calls Lisa. "Mom thinks the president is W.C. Fields."

"Maybe I'll try that. I'll imagine this is all a movie from the 1930s. He's gone, right? W.C. Fields is dead?"

8. Time Travel

At work, Lisa's boss calls her into his office. "If the federal plan eventually goes through, best case? We cut back. Worst case …"

Lisa picks up take-out on the way home. She calls Henry, but he doesn't pick up. There's a Willa Cather book on her nightstand. Soon Lisa's in a different century, strolling through a small Nebraska town.

9. Capitulate

One evening Henry leaves his mother to her TV shows and attends a nearby activist meeting.

In a bookstore, ten people sit in folding chairs. Someone gives a speech. "We'll try everything," she says. "Phone calls, marches."

Henry tells the group he wants to help. The speaker invites him for coffee; maybe, she says, they can collaborate. Sitting across from her, he imagines the warmth of her freckled skin. If he were to stay, he could help his mother. He could spend time getting to know this woman.

Later, on the phone, Lisa speaks of ice cream. "I've stopped buying fancy flavors. Vanilla or chocolate is fine." She talks slowly, as if she's running out of words.

The next day, Henry flies home.

10. Reiterate

They're on the couch, together again. Henry reads political commentary on his tablet. Lisa reads a novel.

"Well?" he asks.

"Not as good as her first. And the world?"

"Homophobia and warmongering. Overt racism."

"So, the usual."

"Yes," he says.

Moving closer, he presses his knee against hers. She rests her elbow on his thigh and they go to bed. Breathing into each other, they explore each other's body as if this were sufficient, as if this simple, easily repeated practice were powerful enough to carry them safely into the future. As if they didn't know that in the morning, in the brightly blinding morning, the newspaper would be out there, laying in wait.

Judy Viertel has been published in *Angels Flight - Literary West*, *Identity Theory*, *Gargoyle Magazine*, *Gold Dust*, and *Short Story America: Anthology Five*. One of four moderators currently running the venerable San Francisco Writers' Workshop, in 2014 she was named San Francisco Teacher of the Year.

The Invisible

By Jason Metz

You do not see us, so let me show you. I'll start here, with a needle. First, there's an antiseptic pad to sterilize the injection area, to the left of the belly button, just below a birthmark. The needle is more like a fat pen, a pre-filled syringe encased in plastic with a trigger button at the top. Stand in front of the mirror, shirtless, the needle pressed up against the stomach, hold your breath. Click. It hurts. Not a lot, but enough to know that it's there. It will pass. Ten seconds goes by, a slight gurgling sound as the plunger reaches the end of the barrel, then wait a few seconds more and remember to breathe. Wipe away the droplets of blood. This happens twice a month, on Tuesdays.

The commercial for my medicine has all of the typical scenes you've come to expect from the pharmaceutical industry: people trying to get on with their daily lives. They're packing suitcases and boarding planes. They're sitting in an Adirondack chair by a lake. They're enjoying romantic dinners. These things happen while a hushed voiceover lists the potential side effects: *serious and sometimes fatal infections and cancers, such as lymphoma have happened, as have blood, liver, and nervous system problems, serious allergic reactions, and new or worsening heart failure.* All the good stuff.

None of it phases me. I know what life is like without the medicine. I enjoy packing suitcases and boarding planes and sitting by a lake. The romantic dinners are a little harder to come by, but not for lack of trying. The medicine allows me to try.

What does phase me, is when the commercial airs during football games. Friends, beers, wings. Trying to pretend that the advertisement for my medicine is just another commercial, couched between fast food ads and movie previews. The actors in the commercial represent my reality. This worries me. That the commercial might expose me, that my friends might catch on, that they'll know something is wrong with me. If a deflection is necessary, I'll make a joke and mock the commercial, get a laugh out of the room. Besides, these commercials are unnecessarily cruel reminders. They air at times when I'm trying to forget. When I'm living, trying to enjoy myself, keeping hidden. Sundays are for football. Every other Tuesday is for the needle.

I was born with an auto-immune disorder. There is no cure. For the rest of my life, some form of treatment is necessary. Without it, my quality of life plummets. And aside from all those physical symptoms and side effects, here's what almost nobody tells you: The mental effects can cripple you. They will follow you at every step for the rest of your life. You will not be able to outrun them.

What might happen when you're sick and always will be, is a depression that weaves its way in and out of your life. Sometimes it's just a touch, barely there, you might not even notice it. Other times, it will consume you. It will corrode your needs and values and desires. There will be days that you cannot leave the house. You'll find excuses to not be with friends. You will have great difficulty with intimacy. Those things that seem to come so easily for others. And you might find yourself staring out of a third story window, looking down at the ground, and thinking how easy it could be. Gone.

These might be passing thoughts, not even a suggestion, just more of an option to look at plainly. The fact that these thoughts exist within you is frightening enough, but there they are, so maybe it's best to acknowledge them. Hang on the best you can and let them pass through. Remind yourself, these thoughts are foolish. It's not all that bad.

There are other thoughts, too. For example, someone might come into your life. You might let your guard down, let someone get close. The problem with that is, eventually, you might have to talk about what you want for the future. This is where, if you don't want to lie, if you're strong enough to give the other person the honesty they deserve, you tell them that you *do not* want children. This will be a deal breaker for many. You can tell them the reasons why, that children just aren't for you or that you don't need to create a life to fulfill your own. There is some truth to this, maybe. But here you are, lying to someone you promised you would not lie to. Here you are, lying to yourself. Here is what you will never tell others. Here is the truth: that you're afraid of what you're going to pass down, what's embedded in your DNA. How could you lovingly create a child and knowingly pass on your pain? How could you bear to watch that? How could you ask someone else to do the same?

It's in these passing moments that you realize that every single day, even in the smallest of ways, you deal in terms of life and death, always. You are afraid to create one. You are afraid of your own. It's in these passing moments that you are grateful for the medicine that alleviates your symptoms. It may not make these thoughts go away. But it gives you some distance. You can't outrun these thoughts, but you can stay ahead.

• • •

You do not see us. But we are very much at risk. The Affordable Healthcare Act provides protection for those of us with pre-existing conditions, whether we were born with them or not. And here we are, once again, about to find ourselves at the mercy of the insurance industry. An industry that does not care for us. Without protections in place, they have the power to simply deny us coverage, or charge us exorbitant premiums that we cannot afford. Many of us will be forced to go without coverage, without treatment.

This is how *they* see us: We are ID numbers in a database. We are a math formula. We are X amount of dollars in premiums. We cost Y amount of dollars in treatments. We never come out in the black. The variable in this formula? Being born. Our complicity? To continually exist. In existence? More than 50 million of us.

We don't want you to see us, but if you must, see us for what we are: human.

Don't see us as simple mathematics, as a financial burden, or a losing proposition. We are not disposable.

We are the invisible. We swallow pills and stick ourselves with needles. We are among you. We watch football games and laugh at ourselves on TV. You invite us to your weddings and baby showers and hug us at funerals. We try to be role models to your children. We're your best friends and, like you, we are trying to get through another day. We might not ask you for help because we too often see help as an admission of weakness. We are stubborn. We work so hard for our invisibility.

But know this: We are in grave danger. Know that we are here, alongside you. Know that we need you, now more than ever.

Jason Metz earned an MFA in Creative Writing from the University of California, Riverside. He lives in Somerville, Massachusetts, on the third floor of a triple-decker, on a hill that overlooks the Boston skyline, where he writes at a small wooden desk, resisting.

This essay was previously published online by *Writers Resist.*

Preamble Ramble

By LJ Provost

We the People of—
> No. Not all the people, but ... most of the people.
>> Well ... not most of the people, but ... some of the people.

Wait, wait. ... We the People who *matter*.
Yes. The People who ... are white.
> No. Not all the people who are white ... but ...
> a lot of the people ... who are White.
>> Well, no. ... Not the poor people ... not the ones
>> who do not own land ... the rest of the White People.

Yes. We the White People who matter,
the White Landowners.
>> Well, not all the white people who own land ... but
>> the White People ... who are male.

Yes! We the White Male People Who Own Land
In Order to form … a more perfect union—
> No, not merely a *more* perfect Union.
>
> We must establish justice.

Yes, justice.
Wait. Wait. … Let us make justice … look fair.
>> Yes, and balanced, but not … oh yes, not,
>>
>> to the detriment of
>>
>> We the White Male People Who Own Land.

Justice must look blind … to bind mistrust … and must,
yes, must look feminine.
> Look feminine to appease … and …
>
> silence our wives.
>
> Yes. That will insure domestic tranquility.

Wait, wait. … Not tranquility … per se.
>> What we want is servility for it is …
>>
>> acknowledged … that
>>
>> We the White Male People Who Own Land …
>>
>> are wise.
> Yes. And powerful.
>
> We seek servility over tranquility
>
> to insure our ability to secure stability,
>
> our stability and gentility.

We the White Male People Who Own Land will defend our status
and extend welfare … to serve and secure
our own best interest.
> Liberty is … our certain unalienable Right ordained … and

reconstituted for us and our Posterity.

No, not all of our posterity ... but—

A lot of our posterity.

Well, not most ... of our posterity.

Wait, wait. ... The Posterity ... who matter.

Yes. The White Male Posterity

of We the White Male People Who Own Land,

that Posterity.

And having established this common
understanding

for the good of our order,

WE THE WHITE MALE PEOPLE WHO OWN LAND DO HEREBY
CLAIM ...

A former journalist and public relations professional, LJ Provost now writes for a government agency to help disaster survivors access assistance. Her work has been published in newspapers, magazines and literary journals. In 2014, she wrote a local history book about Jacksonville, Florida, for Arcadia Publishing. She is pursuing an MFA in Fiction from University of California Riverside-Palm Desert. When she isn't chasing disasters, LJ lives in Jacksonville with a Jack Russell rescue named Nike, who, it turns out, rescued her.

When Our Culture Is Los Angeles Instead of Joshua Tree, This Is How We Elect a President

By Peter Brown Hoffmeister

Part I

Sunrise, the first day in Joshua Tree, a Purple-Bibbed Hummingbird
flits and dips into the late March blooms off my back patio, and a
male House Finch,
head red as a carpet in Hollywood, chatters with his mate about
mosquito meals and black-fly bacon for breakfast.
I turn and watch a jackrabbit facing west, somnolent on his haunches,
the dark tips of his ears catching the first warm rays angling across
the desert, when a raven plunges to him, dives to within a foot of his head,
catches the rabbit staring off, and the rabbit jumps, or—more accurately—
jigs, startles, his four jackrabbit feet spraddling in the air, straight
out to the sides, before he reconnects with the earth and bounds
into the Cliffrose and Saltbush.

At Macy's, this week, in Los Angeles, fur coats are 30% off.

Part II

First night in Joshua Tree, the stars shift counter-clockwise around
Polaris—
Capella, Cassiopeia, and Ursa Major—but also
stars and clusters I haven't yet learned, 3/4 hydrogen, 1/4 helium
thrown from God's bag, 6000 visible above the Lost Horse Cabin on
any given night. But only 119 miles away
in Los Angeles, the burning wattage of the city pollutes a ground-up
whitewash,
as if the people who worship concrete
have painted the sky as nothing.

I've heard *aspiring* actors, *aspiring* directors, and *aspiring* producers
talk about what
they've gained by moving to Los Angeles.

Part III

Cap Rock, walking barefoot back to my car, Cholla spines in the sand
and I shuffle
my feet to scuff the spines so they won't stick.
A coyote yips in front of me, and I try to translate
his yawping whoops,
March Madness, the basketball experts say, would you take Kentucky
or the field?
And I say this is the field, right?
Joshua Tree?
Open desert at 4000 feet through the Lost Horse Valley? The coyote
in front of me still, luring me further into the desert, to a pile
of stones I don't recognize. I follow his yowls for a mile, but

he stays in front of me until
this moment,
now
when coming around a corner to a jamble of orange monzogranite,
he's
in front of me, sitting like a domesticated dog, and I say,
"What was your trick, Trickster?"
But he says, "With them, I didn't have to. Not at all. People,
they just tricked themselves."

Part IV

Finally, An Ode to the Red Carpet Itself:

How did you get this job, not a green or blue carpet. Purple
is a royal color and could be the carpet of choice for
stars to stumble across, bubbly and buzzing from limo shots, or
almost stars—the nearly famous—hoping for interviews, cameras,
microphones,
anything to reflect their own silicon-enhanced images.
Our president is orange but he was once on that reality show where he
always said, "You're fired!" so emphatically that he must be able to
be a boss
win a game
lead a nation
which is synonymous with
starring in a movie?

If you want to catch a raccoon near a desert spring, drive three-inch
nails, angled down,
into a two-pound coffee can, then place something shiny in the bottom:

a silver dollar

a bracelet

a small mirror.

The raccoon, masked and striped as if he's dressed for a special occasion

will grasp the sparkling object in his small dark hand and he won't let go, not even after

he discovers that he can't remove his fist from the trap. Never will this raccoon relinquish the shiny piece of something that he is holding even if he realizes that he

has been caught out in the open, looking like a fool.

Peter Brown Hoffmeister is a poet, memoirist, and fiction author, and a former Writer-In-Residence of Joshua Tree National Park. His most recent novels include *This Is the Part Where You Laugh* (Knopf, Random House) and *Graphic the Valley* (Tyrus Books, Simon & Schuster). His next novel, *Too Shattered for Mending*, was released by Knopf in September 2017.

This poem was previously published online by *Writers Resist.*

Bigotry

bigotry: intolerance of those perceived to be different from oneself

bigot: oh, the many names that come to mind

The Wall, on the preceding page, is by Tomaso Marcolla, born in 1964, in Trento, Italy, where he currently lives and creates. Graduated from the Art Institute of Trento, he began work as a graphic designer in 1985. Marcolla finds digital art is well suited to the frenzy of the current times. The right to employment, the economic crisis, solidarity, nonviolence, the preservation of the environment: the subjects and inspirations of Marcolla's cartoons come from the current news. His posters, created by assembling graphic techniques, photography and computer graphics, have received international awards. He's a member of the AIAP (Italian Association for the Planning of Visual Communication) and the BEDA (Bureau of European Designers Associations). Visit his website at www.marcolla.it.

Breakfast

By Amanda Gomez

The couple next to me is finishing their breakfast.
Between a bite of grits and eggs, the woman asks:
how do they let in trash like that these days? staring

at the television screen, where clips of protestors
gathered at the Trump Tower flash across.
The news anchor covering the story chuckles

nervously, as an interviewee raises the topic of race.
She blushes as if it's inappropriate. *Maybe
I shouldn't be talking about politics* the lady beside me

continues. When her husband makes no response,
she turns towards me. I keep my mouth shut; put myself
in her place. I wonder what would make her America

great again. I think of my mother, my grandmother
and her sisters: where they were when they realized
they were uninvited guests. As for me,

I was in line for recess. A boy called me *spic*
in the third grade. I didn't know what it meant.
If I did I would have called him *caulkie* back.

Let him have it; ensure he never used that word
with me again. It's moments like this still happening,
happening right now, which is why I refuse to respond

when she wants me to engage.
It's simple: I want her to know
that what she's searching for, she can't have.

Amanda Gomez is an MFA candidate in poetry at Old Dominion University. Her work has been published by *Eunoia Review, Ekphrastic Review, Manchester Review, Expound Magazine, San Pedro River Review,* and *Avalon Literary Review.*

This poem was previously published online by *Writers Resist.*

The Daylight Underground

By Héctor Tobar

For the last time, we share a moment of sensual repose. My hand in yours. The sweat on our bare skin, a salty moistness in the desert air. My mestiza, Maritza Melanie. And me, your James, your lover for one hour more.

We weren't supposed to happen. That chance meeting at the political sociology symposium, at the gloriously plain and functional Ramada Inn of Cabrillo, California. If I had turned to the right instead of the left after making my presentation ("The Voting Patterns of Latino Millennials in Suburbia: A Los Angeles Case Study") we would have never been. I'll remember that first lunch and the sudden exchange of intimate stories, the dramedy of our family lives: my absent mother, your oddball father. And that first kiss on your couch, and our lustful fingers and palms, and much later the long walks in search of flora and fauna on the trash-strewn hills above Los Angeles, you showing me the routes the Spanish explorers took, the gathering places of the cholos and the homeless.

Now our final decision as a couple. Do we part ways here, and say our goodbyes at this Tucson hotel? Or do you risk coming with me to the collection point a few blocks away? The risk being that some knucklehead federal officer will see us and smirk at us, and steal that one last thing that belongs only to us. Our farewell caress, the last physical expression of our love. That bond with you that has become as much a part of my being as my citizenship once was. Now the object of his uniformed amusement, his official disdain.

I try not to think the worst of people. A basic politeness is all I ask. But all the kindness is draining from the world. We are too frayed, too harried, too angry, too rushed.

"You need to go," Maritza says.

"Come with me."

"I can't. We discussed this."

"Just walk alongside me."

"If they see me with you. … They have cameras."

"We'll keep a distance."

My own theory about the Powers That Be is that they're less precise and all-seeing than we give them credit for. A million deportations requires blunt bureaucratic instruments, the systematic feeding of names into databases. Persistence, not precision. An army of thick-skulled federal agents and underpaid police officers. Not drones or surveillance. Maritza and her merry band of Pinot-swilling pranksters could start making bombs and those buffoons wouldn't notice. Not that she and her friends are actually planning such a thing. Assorted acts of defiance is all. Spray-painted slogans scribbled on walls at midnight. Messages of resistance delivered artistically, à la Banksy. Surprise shit-pie attacks on the faces of assorted fascist tastemakers, pundits, and politicos: probably a felony, or soon will be. Fecal assault. I worry for Maritza when I hear her talk about these secret actions. And I worry for her now, as I pick up my suitcase and stand next to her.

Before I open the door I present myself to her. My about-to-be-exiled countenance. My belongings: the one bag allowed per regulations, in compliance with the size requirements. Here I am, Maritza. Reach for me, touch me. She reads my thoughts and holds my paler face with her darker hands and kisses me slowly, and our tongues and lips intermingle, and our entire 18-month love affair, beginning to end, is alive in that moment, until salty tears are dripping into our mouths and we step back and wipe off our faces on our sleeves and I open the door.

"I'll walk ahead of you. Follow me," she says. "Just a bit behind. And when you get there we can look at each other, at least."

"I don't think I'll be able to bear that. Seeing you and not touching you."

"We need to be strong. We need to remember everything we can about this day. The injustice of it. It will make us stronger."

"OK." And now I kiss her on the cheek. "Goodbye lover."

"No, not goodbye."

She steps ahead of me in her vermillion corduroys, and I follow the movement of her hips and thighs, and I feel a twinge of desire, and then a heaviness in my chest, and finally I remember a spinning slot-machine of Maritza moments. Her coffee-table and lecture-hall brilliance, the intelligent eyes I can't see. What will she become without me? This is all going to get serious. For her, here, in this crumbling country. Suffering from a chronic case of "convulsiveness," the word Walt Whitman used to describe the U.S.A. before the Civil War. Arguments over slavery that finally ended with fields and fields of dead. "At some point, you're going to need some hard people to help you," I told Maritza just last week. "It may come to that." When history gets truly fucked up, idealists make common cause with street brawlers. In the French Revolution, Danton and his buddies channeled the anger of the unpredictable and violent mobs of Paris. Nelson Mandela was a heavyweight boxer and he started the Spear of the Nation with a few hard-as-nails dudes offering essential assistance. Not that I have any experience in this myself. I've just read about it in books.

One million deportations requires blunt bureaucracy. Persistence, not precision.

There are more people on the street walking alongside us now, and none of them look hard. Like me, they've acquiesced. We accept a short bus ride into Mexico today, instead of a year in jail making hopeless appeals followed by this same trip to Mexico. It's easier, just get it over with. My people are like that. We're all late to our appointment, too. The bus delayed us, the flight delayed us, who gives a fuck? The government is happy to have our unpunctual but deportable bodies. Walking alone, walking in pairs. Carrying suitcases and backpacks. In mine: the embroidered vest I wore when I proposed to Maritza and books. Curiously enough, mostly Latin American authors in English translation. Bolaño, Cortázar, Lispector. And my New Oxford American Dictionary, Fourth Edition. "You're taking a dictionary with you? Shouldn't it be a Spanish dictionary at least?" In our hotel room, between our lovemaking sessions, I opened up my Oxford and looked longingly at my favorite words, like a man studying his children's faces for the last time before they head out to college. Prolix. Praxis. And my Dictionary of American Idioms, "impossible to find in Mexico," I tell her, with gems like "whitewash" and "the whole kit and caboodle."

"You're such a nerd, James," Maritza said with a laugh from the bed, pulling a sheet up over her. "A word nerd."

We reach the address listed on my summons. It's a fenced-off asphalt lot, with a few Tucson police patrols hovering on the perimeter, and a fleet of Customs and Border Protection vans parked nearby, and CBP agents standing by some tables at the entrance to the lot. Maritza, still walking in front of me, makes a slow turn and gives me a sidelong glance with her eyes cast downward. I almost brush against her back as I walk past.

I stand in line and take in the sorrowful tableau. Families gathering to say farewell, lined up on the sidewalk across the street, a few holding medals of Catholic saints. They mourn as if we were dying, and maybe a part of us is. I think I recognize this one guy ahead of me in line. Smart eyes, wrestler's biceps, tall. Yeah, he's the manager at my Jiffy Lube. Suddenly everyone around me looks familiar. The dude with the wispy mustache, can't be older than 30—I've seen him skateboarding on Figueroa. All of us here are from the 90042 ZIP code. The undesirable All-Stars of Northeast Los Angeles, bad hombres and sassy señoritas together one last time as we bid our country adieu. The young woman behind me and the erudite message on her T-shirt: "History is a nightmare from which I am trying to awake." Smart aleck, Occidental College undergrad probably; she makes the rest of us into a piece of performance art illustrating her message. "Marx?" I ask her. "No, Joyce," she says. Ah, an English major, that's why I didn't recognize her. They're not deporting housekeepers any more, just the troublesome overeducated "anchor babies" like me and this Oxy chick. Actually, no. That lady further back. I remember seeing her walk up the hillsides to the fancier houses, very mexicana, pobrecita, going home now. Don't take it so hard, señora, you're not alone. See?

I decide to take a deep, contemplative breath, and consider this undoubtedly bleak historical moment. My professional observation as a political scientist? The obvious: We're a wounded community. The soon-to-be deported ripped from the people we're leaving behind. An old tree with deep and twisted branches, now being sawed through, from top to bottom. The severed bonds of mothers, uncles, sisters, cousins, lovers, and soulmates. I feel our shared nobility, the mixed Mesoamerican-Iberian-Afro-Saxon complexity of us, our twisted bilingual tongues and our triple-tangled DNA, our romantic Latino subconscious and our North American Anglo hang-ups. In our daydreams, we worry. Yes, the Mexican food will we better (by definition); but will we find a decent Starbucks over there, on the other side?

Another professional observation: In the valleys beyond Tucson, the flow still runs northward. Our people are coming here, still somehow smuggling their Spanish-speaking selves over walls, through moats and past motion detectors. Risking their lives for jobs grilling burgers and scrubbing bathrooms. Someone has to do it. They will be living harder lives on this side of the border, undocumented laborers laboring in plain sight, deeper in the daylight underground.

"You'll be back, Matt," I hear a lady yell across the street. "You'll be back."

"I love you Grandma!" Matt yells back.

I reach the front of the line, and the agent inspects my papers.

"Birthplace," he asks me.

"Pasadena, California. U.S.A."

The agent is a big white man who looks embarrassed and/or put out beneath his layers of wool and Kevlar. Maybe he's nostalgic for the Fourteenth Amendment, too. "Your passport?"

"I gave it to the judge." He nods and inspects my California Driver's License, my summons, and gives them both back to me as he punches a few buttons into a mobile device. He waves me forward, through an opening in the fence, into a holding pen. They've found an appropriately barren and ugly location in this otherwise pleasant desert city in which to rustle us together. A last vacant, weed-filled lot at the end of our American road.

"This is so fucked up," the Jiffy Lube manager says to me. He lights a cigarette and offers me one. No thanks. Several other people have started to puff away, and their tobacco smoke forms a series of exclamation points over their nicotine-soothed heads until a soft breeze comes through and the smoke serpentines into question marks. I look through the fence, across the street, and I find Maritza's face. Wearing shades, of course. My spy, undercover in her Ray-Bans. Or is it so I can't see her tears?

"This is a nonsmoking area!" one of the agents says. Federal regulations, you know.

"What are you gonna do, deport us?" the Jiffy Lube guy says, and everyone keeps smoking.

I look over at the line and my eye is drawn to a tall woman near the front. Black, straight hair falling over her face. She looks up to wipe her tears. Oh shit! No fucking way! It's Katarina Consuelo Ramirez. Los Angeles City College adjunct, and my fiery, passionate, and deeply disturbed ex. Known as Kat-Con to her many fans and detractors in the small and incestuous circle of untenured Latino political scientists. Kat-Con, my intimidatingly beautiful partner for two years and Maritza's nemesis since grad school at Berkeley. Kat-Con with her high cheekbones, the tiny exotic bump in her nose, has many eyes falling upon her. She's not carrying a single piece of luggage. Not even a purse, as if she were here to model Southwestern eco-fashions. I am Kat-Con, a martyred second-generation Honduran immigrant deportee of Los Angeles: Yes, you may take a picture of me, of the glorious, tragic beauty of my stripped citizenship, with this carefully chosen cashmere scarf against the winter desert chill. She looks up from the agent's desk and walks into the holding pen and she spots me, and hugs me, and she buries her head in my chest.

"Oh, James. Look at us."

No, look at Maritza, says the voice in my head. So I do. My fiancée has lifted up her shades in shock. From across the street and through the fence she's mad-dogging me. I see her mouthing words. I'm not a great lip reader, but I'm pretty sure it's: "How could you?" followed by "You son of a bitch." As if I'd arranged my deportation so that I could have a tryst with my ex. With Kat-Con still embracing me, I raise my arms and shrug my shoulders as if to say, *How could I know?*

I see Maritza turning away, leaving the crowd of onlookers, headed back to her car at the hotel parking lot, no doubt. And now the thought hovers over me. That my Maritza will write me off, forget me, assuming me happily reborn into a Mexicanness I've never truly known, content and coital on the other side of the border in the arms of Kat-Con. No. This can't be. I feel the absurdity and an emptiness all at once. In the name of Thomas Jefferson, Clarence Darrow, and Oscar Zeta Acosta, no! This is one crazy and unfair thing too many. So I break free from Kat-Con's tearful embrace and push through the crowd to the opening in the fence and the desk, and back out into free Tucson, with the CBP agent behind me yelling, "Hey where the fuck are you going?" And for the three seconds it takes me to cross the street everyone around me—my fellow deportees, Kat-Con, the families on the sidewalk, the Tucson police, and the Customs and Border Protection agents—are all frozen in place, and only I am moving toward the departing Maritza, whose back is still facing me.

"Maritza!" I yell, and she turns, looking at me in confusion, and before she can say anything I've got my arms around her, and I'm saying "I love you I love you I love you," and she whispers "I know you do," and of course we kiss. An illicit, public meeting of our lovers' lips, with 100 people and unseen cameras watching. The street and sidewalk around us erupt with appreciative sighs and laughter. I hear ranchera whoops, and catcalls, and a "who-who-whoey!" and an "órale!" It's as if we were back home in a bar on York Boulevard— before the bars got gentrified. But now the desk agent is walking toward us, and he's got a baton in his hands. I am about to raise my arms in surrender, when I see Kat-Con running behind him. In that instant I remember that she was once a taekwondo instructor in Oakland, and I watch as she grabs the agent by the shoulders from behind and uses her hands, arms, and legs to expertly separate his feet from gravity. He falls heavily and beefily to the asphalt.

Now that's a tough woman. But is this "political" Kat-Con, in full militant mujer mode, in a final act of defiance against the machinery of hate? Or is this a Kat-Con who once carried a torch for me? Or is it just the impulsive, crazy Kat-Con who got fired from Cal State Dominguez Hills after she screamed at the dean? Or maybe it's all those Kat-Cons at the same time. As two CBP agents rush toward Kat-Con and their fallen colleague, a few of the deportees in the pen start climbing the flimsy fence holding them in, and the fence falls, and several of them run across it to kiss and hug their lovers and their mothers. Kat-Con breaks free of the confused and distracted agents. She begins running down the street with long strides, and she turns to flip the bird to the agents and their smashed holding pen. Then she is gone around the corner, free.

"It's a riot," Maritza says. A riot of kisses, hugging, wrestling, prayers, sirens, and shouts.

I take Maritza by the hand and we start to run, spontaneously, without thinking about it, as if running were a behavior written deep in the code of our being.

"We're fucked," Maritza says a block into our sprint.

"But we're free," I answer.

We run one or two blocks more. And then we walk. Normally, as if nothing were amiss, as if one or both of us wasn't a felon. Back into the daylight underground, where we will remain. Waiting for the data miners and the drones to catch up with us. Maybe this afternoon, maybe tomorrow. Maybe never. We turn a corner, taking a zigzagging route toward Maritza's car even though no one is following us. We reach a big, open lot of sandy ground with a single huge cactus in the center. "Whoa," Maritza says. "Look at this." We admire the plant and the weird, prickly, tangled snakes of its many arms. We stand there, in the crisp sunshine of Arizona winter, and take a moment to hold hands in its holy presence. Maritza says it's probably 100 years old, and as we continue our journey I think about all the decades it's survived, all the droughts and the floods, growing gnarly limbs, pushing roots into the desert soil.

Héctor Tobar's most recent books are *Deep Down Dark: The Untold Stories of 33 Men Buried in a Chilean Mine and the Miracle That Set Them Free*, which was a finalist for the National Book Critics Circle Award, and *The Barbarian Nurseries*, which won the California Book Award Gold Medal for Fiction.

This short story was previously published by *Slate* in The Trump Story Project and by *Writers Resist* online.

Land of the Free

By Sahar Fathi

You say
we are all equal
Give us your tired
your poor
your huddled freaking masses!
But not if
they are Muslim
brown
persecuted
by governments (we installed)
drug wars (we created)
I say
give them to me
I will pull the stars from the sky
to light their way
o'er the land of the free
and whisper to them
of the America we can be

Sahar Fathi is the Division Director for Leadership Development at the Department of Neighborhoods in the City of Seattle. Sahar graduated from the University of Washington Law School and is a member of the New York bar. She has a Masters in International Studies from the University of Washington and a dual Bachelor of Arts in French and International Relations from the University of Southern California. Sahar has worked on immigrant and refugee issues for more than ten years. She has served as adjunct faculty at Seattle University and the University of Washington School of Law, and she has been published in the *Seattle Journal for Social Justice*, the *Seattle Journal of Environmental Law*, and the *Gonzaga Law Review*. Following President Trump's Executive Orders banning travel from majority Muslim countries, Sahar volunteered at SeaTac airport to support impacted travelers. In her spare time, she enjoys exploring resistance through Iranian cooking. Follow her on Instagram at @sfathis.

This poem was previously published by *Writers Resist*.

lavender:

By Lily Moody

Pink or blue

When our daughters are taught to hold their tongues and our sons are taught to hold their tears, when all we want to do is scream and sob.

Pink or blue

When dolls and toy trucks, bows and baseball gloves are used as barriers to separate us,
when femininity and masculinity are shamed from crossing paths.

Pink or blue

When the blood pumps the same through all bodies and these bones cage a fire so much brighter than they will ever begin to understand.

When he paints his lips dark red and finally feels beautiful, when she lets the hair on her body grow into a forest.

Lily Moody is a former yet-to-be-published writing student and an activist, located in Southern New Hampshire and hoping to make a difference through poetry and prose.

This poem was previously published online by *Writers Resist*.

On Learning the Department of Justice, Using an Artistic Expression Argument, Will Side With the Colorado Baker Who Refused to Sell a Wedding Cake to a Same-Sex Couple

By Joni Mayer

The baker is open to the public,
may have asked his other couples
how and where they met—eHarmony,
blind date, a Boulder bar, but never Grindr—
may have been inspired by those data to use
apricot filling in place of peach mousse,
to stack four tiers instead of three,
may have lied under oath to veil his hate
when he said he'd sold gay folks *birthday* cakes
and *retirement* cakes. *Artistic expression,* this reason
will melt in a higher court like buttercream frosting
in the afternoon heat.
A cake is not a poem.

Joni Mayer grew up in Birmingham, Alabama, and has lived in San Diego, California, since 1986. After a 30-year career in academia focusing on health behavior research, she retired early to return full time to the world of poetry. Her poems have appeared in *AURA Literary Arts Review*, *Eckerd Review*, *San Diego Poetry Annual* and *Acorn Review*.

This poem was previously published online by *Writers Resist*.

Whatever Happened to Brian?

By Kit-Bacon Gressitt

It was a blustery Santa Ana afternoon when Rose Kaminski, a petite octogenarian, encountered the stranger at Persimmon and Main, in lovely downtown Fallbrook. She'd asked the pasty schmuck for help at the crosswalk, but he'd blocked her path and argued against her pursuit.

"God knows what might have happened if you hadn't come by," Rose said to the Eagle Scout who'd rescued her. She smiled at a handful of folks, halfheartedly attracted to what could barely be considered a ruckus—but it was something to do. They all watched the unpleasant man galumph to the next property, stoop, and occupy himself with a pocket gopher hole where the sidewalk met the yard's edge.

"I only asked him for an arm to lean on, to get across the street," Rose explained, "but he refused to help me! 'I reject your request,' he said, 'I strike it down.' Crazy nincompoop."

The curious pedestrians nodded in agreement and murmured sounds of displeasure.

Rose was glad she'd dolled up before her errand; you never know when you'll have an audience. She wore her finest polyester pantsuit—mint-green—and sneaks, the balls of her Peds, a perfectly matching hue. Rose knew she looked just lovely.

"It's a special day for me, you see. But my, oh my, that man nearly jumped out of his skin when I asked for his help. I told him I was meeting my beloved to pick up our marriage license. Oy, the putz! I guess he's not used to folks being friendly—this *is* Fallbrook the Friendly Village, don't you know."

Heads again bobbed and the displeasure became more distinct.

"The audacity," a ramrod volunteer from the library said.

"What kinda guy does that?" another of the sidewalk congregants asked.

"Oughta run him out of town," said the disheveled young woman, known for collecting discarded bottles roadside and howling with the coyotes in the dead of night.

"Maybe, maybe." Rose chuckled as she tucked a folded Macy's shopping bag under one green arm and with the other hand clasped the Eagle Scout's elbow. They began a slow toddle across the street. "Between us—shush, now, you didn't hear this from me—that unhelpful man favors the Pillsbury Dough Boy, don't you know, bubele."

"Bubba what?" the scout asked. "Is that, like, Jewish?"

"No—that's bu-be-le—I grew up in Brooklyn. My Frankie, rest his soul, brought us out to Fallbrook to develop a blight-resistant avocado. He did like to tinker. And look at you. Aren't you a nice young man to help an old lady. I can tell it's going to be another fabulous Fallbrook afternoon."

The nice young man said nothing else, eager to perform his good deed and get on with being a teenager. The poor boychick, Rose noticed, was devastated by pronounced acne. A little chicken soup, maybe, she wondered, heals a multitude of sins.

When they reached the other side, she posed to give him her

traditional peck on the cheek, but thought better of it and squeezed his arm instead.

"Thanks, my boy. Toot-a-loo."

While she continued her way to Town Hall, musing over the pocket gopher fancier, little did she know the handful of folks was growing in number and insight.

"Who was that jerk?" one of the newly gathered asked.

"He's that Brian Brown guy—saw his bus around the corner—from National Organization for Marriage."

"The guy was gonna save us from gay marriage way back when?"

"That ship's sailed—into Rainbowland."

"Yeah, my kid's on it."

"Mine, too. She's the captain, and I'm proud of her!"

"So what's the jerk want now?"

"And why didn't he just help the lady cross the street?"

"An outrage, is it, an outrage!"

"Goddamn un-Christian, too."

"Throwing that lady's harmless request into a dustbin, like she was trash."

"Like his self-importance should trump her plea for help!"

"You gotta point: Must be Trump's fault."

"That's not what I mean—"

"What's with this guy, anyway? Why'd he do it?"

The grumbling group turned from the corner to glare at the man still pretending fascination with the rodent hole.

"Brian, hey Brian!" they called to him. "You must explain yourself."

Brian, sensing an unreceptive audience, considered turning tail and running like hell to his *Spring for Marriage 2018: One Man, One Woman of Child-Bearing Age* tour bus, but he took so long to consider his exit that he was surrounded before he could push his quads into a standing position.

The group had become a crowd, thanks to the residents of the Shady Oaks Rest Home. They'd just hit the street for their daily power walk and, sharing a predilection for sucking up local gossip, they wanted in on whatever was happening. Even the pizza guy had stopped mid-delivery to see what was up. Fallbrook could be pretty boring.

Brian eyed the fomenting mass, whispered a prayer, stood and said, "I'll take your questions now."

"How could you refuse what I'm told was a pretty benign request, Brian?" asked Jorge Adams, an adjunct professor of philosophy at the local Cal State. At the moment, though, he was moonlighting as a skateboarding pizza delivery guy, a pragmatic strategy he hoped to abandon if he could get just one more class. "All that sweet gal wanted was a little help off the curb, Brian. And on her special day! Don't you aspire to a higher plane? What gives, man?"

Brian put his right hand to his heart, his polling having indicated that 67 percent of respondents interpreted the gesture as strongly positive.

"Now, let me just preface this with my absolute assurance that I bear no ill will toward senior citizens," Brian intoned. "I harbor no prejudice in my heart. I have senior citizens who are friends and family. Nonetheless, that woman is headed to meet her partner at Town Hall, to apply for a marriage license, and that jeopardizes the traditional definition of marriage across this great nation of ours. Why, senior-citizen marriage is threatening to strip millions of Americans of our right to traditional marriage!"

"Oh, yeah?" the philosophic pizza person asked as he passed out slices to calm the restless gawkers. "How so?"

"Senior-citizen marriage is unfruitful. It will undermine the institution of marriage as we've known it for millennia. We must make it clear to activist judges and the out-of-control Congress:

Senior-citizen marriage conflicts with marriage's central purpose—procreation."

A sense of unease spread through the retirees, although more than a few couples took advantage of the pressing pack to cop a feel or two.

"Well, yep, she looked a bit too mature to have a bun in the oven." Jorge twirled an empty pizza box on one finger while the crowd applauded politely, until a burst of Santa Ana wind carried it away. "But you haven't answered my question, Brian. How is senior-citizen marriage threatening what you call *traditional* marriage? That smacks of a non sequitur. Maybe it's time for you to pack up this crusade and get a real job, man. They're hiring at Itza Pizza."

"But the sheer audacity of senior citizens, denying the procreational purpose that marriage is intended for, one husband, one wife, uh—procreating. We must protect traditional marriage from— protect it from— from them!" He jerked his head at the people circling him.

The people growled.

"Brian, you're not making one iota of sense, dude." Jorge sucked some pizza sauce from the COEXIST tie his former wife had given him for Co-parents Day, and a low rumble filled the silence. He handed out more pizza and said, "Brian, you're stuck in an irresolvable rut of your own making. Climb out, man, before it's too late."

"But, but—"

"Look, Brian, there's no way you're going to stop seniors from being married. Come on now, guy! They might be a little wrinkled, there is that talcum powder smell, but they're still human beings. They deserve the same rights as the rest of us."

"Yeah, that!" the people chimed in amid the heightening rumble. The calming influence of mozzarella was wearing off.

Brian eyed the riled folks and his sweat glands gushed. "You've got to listen to me. Marriage is the exclusive right of a man and a woman for the purpose of procreation. It's what's best for children, for families, for the nation!" He pulled a handkerchief from his pocket and sopped the salty flow at his chin. "Senior citizens, well, they're— an abomination. They're too old for—" He scrunched his eyes shut and moaned.

The assembly drew a collective gasp—that he was imagining them *in flagrante* was grossing them out.

"Damn voyeur!" They shook their fingers at Brian.

"Punk ass chump!" snarled one particularly active but non-procreative couple.

"Brian, Brian, Brian." Jorge patted the charged air. "Get your mind out of the gutter. Pay attention to the stats. We are an aging population. Don't mess with the dominant demographic's sexual pleasures. It's Baby Boomers, man. They might be cruising into their golden years, but they're still having plenty of nookie."

"Euww!" Brian shuddered.

The crowd cheered, a lot of winking and backslapping ensued, and the wind captured one man's dime-store toupee, but he was having too much fun being annoyed by the punkster to go after it.

Brian groaned. "No, no! It's—disgusting—death knell of traditional marriage—how can they?—unthinkable—Grams and Granny going at it?—God almighty, it's—gyuhhchgchchch!!"

And that was more than the people would tolerate. The rumble erupted from the depths of the throng, howling and shrieking. Jorge, an intuitive philosopher, leapt from its center as an explosion of enraged people swarmed Brian, who disappeared beneath a battering of knock-off purses, rolled newspapers, wads of Indian casino flyers, and well-aimed Shady Oaks water bottles.

Jorge thought about stepping back into the fray to intervene, but decided to let natural law run its course. Besides, he had to get over to Itza Pizza and explain the unpaid consumption of five extra-larges.

He skated out of sight, the mob thinned, and Rose returned, her hand on the arm of a hefty, sweet-faced man. "Did we miss something?" she asked the stragglers.

"Not much," said Rod *The Rod* Robertson, a retired professional wrestler and occasional birthday party clown. "We just took care of some pipsqueak senior citizenphobe."

"That nebbish who wouldn't help me across the street? I told you about him, Bruno. His poor mother, what a disappointment, what a heartache." She patted her fiancé's arm—"Not like my Bruno"—and gave him a peck on the cheek.

"Yes, sweetie." Bruno gave her a reciprocal kiss.

"You look lovely today, Rose," The Rod said, shuffling his feet and mourning Bruno's success.

"Thank you, Rod," Rose squeezed his arm. "Aren't you a dear. See you in the dining room?"

She waved and walked on with Bruno, arm in arm. "It takes all kinds, don't you know, but between us, bubele—shush, now, you didn't hear this from me—that young man favored the Pillsbury Dough Boy."

"Yes, sweetie, I'd wager he did." Bruno had already heard the story twice before, but he knew how to make an old gal feel good. He gave her a love pinch. "Rosie, would you like to take a little nap before the wedding, sweetie?"

"Don't you know I would." Rose giggled.

While she and Bruno teetered up the flagstones to Shady Oaks' front door, a Santa Ana gust lifted an abandoned pizza box, still bearing a few unclaimed slices, spun it into the air and wafted it along the street, dipping and arcing and surfing around the corner. The devil wind plastered it against the side of Brian's bus, smearing pizza sauce across his campaign slogan.

Some weeks later, the local sheriff's station, fed up with multiple complaints, had the bus towed to the impound lot, and the folks at Shady Oaks agreed, it was another fabulous Fallbrook afternoon.

Kit-Bacon Gressitt, a feminist writer, was spawned by a Southern Baptist creationist and a liberal social worker, thus inheriting the requisite sense of humor to survive family dinner-table debates and the imagination to avoid them. A fan of reproductive justice, K-B's had two abortions and one child, a young woman of color who's taught her a lot about intersectionality. After earning an MFA in Creative Writing from University of California Riverside-Palm Desert, K-B taught Women's Studies and managed to get some things published in various literary journals and other outlets, including, *Not My President: The Anthology of Dissent*, *Publishers Weekly*, *Ducts* magazine, *The Missing Slate*, *Trivia: Feminist Voices*, and *Evening Street Review*. She's the publisher and a founding editor of *Writers Resist*.

The Streets

By Raya Yarbrough

My aunt took me down to Harlem, down to Adam Clayton Powell
Jr. Blvd.
She talked to me about history, and struggle,
and my head took it in, as the history of struggle.
And my life went on.
Colorless conversations.
Happy white-noise.
Then I woke up, and her words were not history.
Place your hand on the asphalt.
The streets are hot.
They never cooled.

Raya Yarbrough is a singer and composer from Los Angeles, California.
She is the singer in the opening credits of *Outlander*, and Yarbrough's
original music has also been featured in numerous films and televisions
shows. She has performed/collaborated with pianist Billy Childs and

Van Dyke Parks. After three independent albums and countless live performances, including opening for Terence Blanchard at The Jazz Standard in New York City, Yarbrough made her international debut on Telarc (Concord) with her self-titled album, *Raya Yarbrough*. She is currently in the studio working on an album version of her original musical, *North of Sunset West of Vine*, a spoken-word influenced stage piece about growing up on Hollywood Boulevard in the late 1980s. Visit her website at www.RayaYarbrough.com.

This poem was previously published online by *Writers Resist*.

Declaration of Defendence

By Conney D. Williams

I save my tears for weddings and presidential elections
while America the beneficent thrusts anthems up our spleens
the pasty ballot of deprecation without representation
please GOD, bless Ol' Glory with sufficient stars and stripes
to vandalize my person until even bowels lose their allegiance
I am a casualty of domestic terrorism and
the transparency of America's image casts no reflection
although lynchings are no longer the rage at picnics
state sanctioned genocide statistics suffice
prison systems compete with the Atlantic
for who holds the most slaves on death row
we live in an error of democracy
afflicted dissidents borrow retribution
then blow up U.S. entitlement and self-appreciation
the three blind mice are completely outraged
there is no spare change for self-imposed tragedies
this nation was bankrupt before its depression
misconceived foreign citizens sweated this economy
through the blood and flesh of capitalisms

let me sign, let me sign
please let me sign on that dotted line
let me sign then make my mark
below the signatures of Jefferson and Hancock

silhouettes and profiling require you know your place
so assume the nigga position please
keep your eyes on the national policy
you are getting sleepy and will not see what you really know
clasp your hands behind your head
lift every voice and sing
join in the organ grinder's tune
because this is America's favorite sing-a-long
"o' say can you see by the dawn's early plight"
new political pimps occupy opaque condominiums
federally funded on Pennsylvania Avenue
they pray like pious prostitutes but don't use condoms
they train and arm their adversaries to kill their offspring
we are third world soldiers who don't cry in public
mis-taken identity is what aborts freedom
the national opinion is infected by syphilis of patriotism
preaching the eminent eulogy for just-us
we are the offspring of Emmett Till, and
still breathe the muddy water of his incarnation
the purple color of our tattered existence
is the congealed breath of intended victims

let me sign, let me sign
please let me sign on that dotted line
let me sign then make my mark
below the signatures of Jefferson and Hancock

we are America's unsolved national homicide
where is the milk carton campaign to locate lost ancestors
their admonition is forget your holocausts
and continue to smile for the camera
while the republic eats its young to support humanitarian efforts
balance the budget for their domestic foreign policies
in order to sacrifice their homegrown aliens
this is the bastard image of U.S. hypocrisy
but things will be different
when we get back to normal
things will be different
when we get back to those ideals
of the baby daddies of the constitution
then I remember
that we didn't have founding fathers
only mother-fuckers

let me sign, let me sign
please let me sign on that dotted line
let me sign then make my mark
below the signatures of Jefferson and Hancock
let me sign on that dotted line

Conney D. Williams is a Los Angeles-based poet, actor and performance artist, originally from Shreveport, Louisiana, where he worked as a radio personality. Conney's first collection of poetry, *Leaves of Spilled Spirit from an Untamed Poet*, was published in 2002. His poetry has also been published in various journals and anthologies including *Voices from Leimert Park, America: At the End of the Day*, and *The Drumming Between Us*. His collection *Blues Red Soul Falsetto* was published in December 2012, and he has released two new poetry CDs, *Unsettled Water* and *River&Moan*, available on his website at conneywilliams.com.

This poem was previously published online by *Writers Resist.*

Nightmare on Elm Street

By Cassandra Lane

Dylann Storm Roof invades my dream space in the days after he murders nine African Americans at a Bible study in Charleston, South Carolina.

His spirit travels 2,480 miles to reach the interior of my imagination in Los Angeles. Like a bloodhound, he finds my Southern black body hiding out in the desert. As though terrorizing his victims and their families were not enough, as though destroying the sanctity of an historically black house of worship were not enough, he comes to me, the girl who grew up kneeling beside her elders in anointed prayer at St. Paul Baptist Church down the street.

Unshackled and smug, he comes to me.

He comes for me. For us.

The dream begins under the cover of night, full of silence and a pregnant, starless sky. My heart pumps into this blackness. The blackness responds, alive and aware.

The scene switches to a clear afternoon, where sunlight slants between two buildings that stand on a hill. I am walking down a slope to pick my son up from school when I catch a glimpse of a man lurking next to a string of parked cars. He is wearing a soiled white t-shirt and jeans. Something in my spirit tells me that this man is wrong. All wrong.

I rush my son home, which turns out to be the home I grew up in on Elm Street in Louisiana. I am back in the South, after all. In the 1980s, this house was the object of constant teasing.

"It's Freddy Krueger's house," the same gaggle of kids would yell day after day when the school bus pulled up to 202 Elm Street. "Yeah, and there's his girlfriend: Frederica!"

In my dream, I pause on the porch to finger the empty spot where the third address number should have been: 20_.

But the gunman is on my trail, so I yank open the front door that was always unlocked, get my son and myself inside and turn the locks. Roof shows up seconds later, trying to get in, rifle in hand.

As my son and I look for safe places to hide, I am both terrified and furious. I am tempted to ignore the possibility of death and unleash my rage on Roof's face, tear at his skin, the mask over hate (what does it look like?).

Roof continues to point his rifle, its snout peering at the front door's window. He could easily shoot out the glass and work his way in. Instead, his strategy is to drag out the terror with painstaking patience and steadiness—tinkering with the door handle, making threats, stopping completely, and then starting up again. I hold the product of terror in my hands; it is in my son's small shoulders. His shoulders are bare and brown, full of naked fear.

I carry his tremors in my fingers, dialing first my husband and then the numbers that I have forgotten to constantly reiterate to my son: 9-1-1. In bursts of hysteria, I appeal to the operator: "He wants to kill us."

"Ma'am," the operator says calmly, "someone is on the way to help you."

When the sheriff shows up, I look out the living room's side window, facing west. The sheriff and Roof stand outside the patrol car, face to face, their arms at their sides, relaxed.

Roof is suddenly in a business suit—navy blue, immaculate. I see his rifle, hiding under the sheriff's car. I hear the sheriff talking to him in a low, calm tone. I make my way outside to get inside this, their intimate conversation.

With a screech, my husband drives up, jumps out of his car and lunges for the terrorist, but I lunge for him to restrain him. I envision the handcuffs glaring against his brown wrists. Click. Guilty. Assault. Attempted murder.

I hold him down and he holds me down, and in this holding we begin, slowly, to regain our composure.

We are statues of self-restraint.

Formerly a newspaper journalist and high school teacher, Cassandra Lane has published essays, columns and articles in *The Times-Picayune, The Source, TheScreamOnline, BET Magazine, The Atlanta Journal Constitution, Bellingham Review* and *Gambit*, and in the anthologies *Everything but the Burden, Ms. Aligned* and *Daddy, Can I Tell You Something*. She is an alum of Voices of Our Nation Arts (VONA) and A Room of Her Own Writing Retreat (AROHO). She received an MFA in creative writing from Antioch University Los Angeles. A Louisiana native, she now lives with her family in Los Angeles.

This essay was previously published online by *Writers Resist*.

Confederate Monument

By Luke A. Powers

High above
Courthouse square

Atop an impossibly
Tall pillar

He has stood
Sentinel now

A hundred years
Summers, winters,

Facing a South
Always farther away

Waiting for word
Signal, reinforcement

Until he's gone
Blind in alabaster

In cap and gloves
His buttons smooth

Leaning on a rifle
That like his face

Is losing definition
The vestige of history

He wants to come down
He can't remember

The high deeds
The sacred cause

The ideas that make
Blood turn to stone

The sky is swept
Clean of martyrs

Clouds fray in bliss
In sweet nothingness

He wants to come down
Laid in cool earth

Like a dark seed that
Will never grow anything

But a deep forgetfulness
Past echoes of rumor

Where none of this
Ever happened

None of this, not
A single minie ball,

Ever was—

But still he stands
At his post

Sun and moon
Unmourned, undead

Waiting only for
This past to be done.

Luke A. Powers teaches English at Tennessee State University, an historically black university in Nashville. He is a singer-songwriter and a member of The Spicewood Seven, who have released two protest albums: *Kakistocracy* (2006) and *Still Mad* (2016), both musical acts of resistance.

This poem was previously published online by *Writers Resist*.

White Privilege

By Keith Welch

the U.S. Caucasian has
a marvelous power

invisible, noticed
only by its absence

subtle in action:

the lack of a shadow
following you through a 7-11

or utterly, terribly clear:

the lack of 19 bullet holes
piercing your body

on the news, you may notice
your senior photo
instead of a mug shot

in the city, the absence
of a cop's hand
in your pockets

in your car, a warning
instead of dying
in a jail cell

there are those who will deny
the power's very existence

it shouts its presence
to those outside its shield

Keith Welch lives in Bloomington, Indiana. He has had work published in Louisville's *Leo* magazine and online at *Spilling Cocoa Over Martin Amis*. Follow him on Twitter @outraged_poet.

This poem was previously published online by *Writers Resist*.

Black Panther vs. the White Bag

By MA Durand

Red hands. White hands. Blue hands. Agents of the White Bag sit idle waiting. Tapping fingers await a panther, a Black Panther snarling, muscles tense. A snarling tense muscled beautiful Black Prince from Oakland by way of NYC, Chicago, Montgomery, Atlanta all points on The BPP.

Tapping fingers rise to cover but the Panther says *black* its shadow captures except for one incognito hand that creeps under the now still hands as it seeks to overlay Black Panther with nothing.

Into nothing at all its ambition—Black Panther reshaped with the mouth of Ben Carson, the eyes of Omarosa, the hands of David Clarke, the feet of Clarence Thomas. Domesticate into dormancy and compliance that Great Black Cat that sits walks ignores snarls pounces creates like all the Great Cats. Black Panther bites the hand that tries to feed it. That Black Cat ain't havin' it—and that's a fact.

MA Durand began writing stories at age seven and is now an undergraduate student, just three credits from earning a BA in Creative Writing with a Concentration in Literature at Antioch University. The writer lives in Barstow, California, which is located in the Mojave Desert, and has traveled overseas and lived in Cairo, Egypt.

Asphalt

By Suzanne O'Connell

Your arms waved for help.
The policeman bent down, hand on gun.
"No!" you shouted.
He fired.
The sound, an exploding beehive.
I looked at your fragile skull, resting
on the sharp leaves of fall.
Your eyelids blinked.

Helicopters circled, sirens came.
Your blood kept pooling.
It was the color of mine.
I saw the snow catch in your curly hair.

You had something in your hand,
a Black Cow caramel bar.
"It Lasts All Day," the wrapper said.

Suzanne O'Connell is a poet and clinical social worker living in Los Angeles, California. Her recently published work can be found in *Poet Lore, American Chordata, Alembic, Forge, Juked, Existere,* and *Crack the Spine.* O'Connell was nominated twice for a Pushcart Prize. Her first poetry collection, *A Prayer for Torn Stocking,* was published by Garden Oak Press in 2016. Visit Suzanne's website at SuzanneOconnell-poet.com.

This poem was previously published online by *Writers Resist.*

Of Gas and Guilt

By Alexander Schuhr

My grandfather farted a lot. Sometimes it took as little as rising from a chair or a slight adjustment of his position and he'd let one fly. In my preadolescent years, I used to burst into laughter. And why not? Among my classmates, a thunderous salute called for proper acknowledgement. Embarrassment was so completely absent that we would occasionally force one out, just to obtain the cheers of adoring fans. But this response to my grandfather's flatulence was not appreciated. Hushing, hissing, and poisonous gazes would hit me and abruptly end my delight. My grandfather's farts were no laughing matter.

Much later, after my grandfather had died, I learned that leg prostheses often produce flatulence sounds. Air is trapped between stumps and prosthetic liners, and its release may sound like a fart. My grandfather had lost a leg above the knee. And while I can certainly not exclude that some of the sounds he produced were the real thing, I was shamed by the insight that I had often ridiculed a humiliating side effect of his handicap.

But neither my grandfather nor any other adult ever bothered clarifying this simple misunderstanding. The reason, I believe, wasn't the poor taste of my reaction. The whole subject of my grandfather's lost leg was off limits. Only at his funeral did my grandmother, no longer in possession of her full mental faculties, reveal the details.

The end of the Second World War was approaching, and allied troops had landed on the beaches of Normandy.

My grandfather sought shelter in in a trench when he spotted a hostile soldier, a few hundred feet away. "I got him," he announced and crawled out of the trench to take aim. Then came the explosion and the shrapnel that hit him. "My leg is gone," he screamed, as he was dragged back into the trench. "Calm down, it's still there," was the response. But my grandfather was right. The impact had severed the bone.

Veterans were wounded, lost limbs, and were mentally scarred by the things they'd seen. But many took comfort in the fact that they'd fought for a good cause: for freedom, for democracy, against tyranny.

There was no such consolation for my grandfather. He had fought for Hitler.

He was only twelve when Hitler came to power. When the Nazis ignited the war, he was old enough to be drafted. Half a century later, I would see his reaction to images on TV, images of the war, images of the genocide committed in the name of German superiority. "We didn't know that," he would mumble, and then change the channel or take another sip from the beer bottle.

It wasn't in him, the extraordinary heroism of resistance that some displayed, often paying the ultimate price. Perhaps he wasn't aware of the extent of the war crimes and atrocities. Maybe he didn't fully understand the meaning of war, what it led to, and how it would eventually ravage his own life. He had been deceived, he would claim.

But there was no deception in the politics that made it all possible. There was no deception in the public display of resentment and chauvinism. The incitement of hatred, the scapegoating of the marginalized, the terrorizing of easy victims—they all had happened out in the open, for many years before the killing began. Many Germans of my grandfather's generation embraced these developments, or, at least, accepted them. And therein lies their guilt.

It was this guilt my grandfather tried to bury, although the guilt stayed, stalking him to his deathbed. It was this guilt that prevented him from mourning, from healing, from finding any meaning in his personal suffering.

Today, resentful politics is on the rise again, and many give in to its cathartic temptations. But the price may be awful, and nothing may ever be innocent again. Not even the silly giggling of an immature boy at the supposed passing of gas.

Alexander Schuhr is an author, essayist and scholar. He was born and raised in Munich, Germany. Before coming to the United States, he lived in various countries in Europe and Sub-Saharan Africa. He holds an M.A. in political science and a Ph.D. in economics. He writes fiction and creative nonfiction. He has a wife and a three-year-old daughter.

This essay was previously published online by *Writers Resist.*

The Night Journey

By Jonathan May

A found poem from: FBI Guantanamo Bay Inquiry // The Night
Journey, Sura 17, The Koran // Department of Defense Human
Resource Exploitation Training Manual – 1983

The purpose of all coercive techniques is to induce psychological regression in the subject by bringing a superior outside force to bear on his will to resist.

on several occasions, witness ("W") saw detainees ("ds") in interrogation rooms chained hand and foot in fetal position to floor w/no chair/food/water; most urinated or defecated on selves, and were left there 18, 24 hrs or more.

Invite men to the way of the Lord, by wisdom, and mild exhortation; and dispute with them in the most condescending manner: For your Lord knows well him who strays from the path, and He knows well those who are rightly directed.

d was kept in darkened cell in Naval Brig at GTMO, then transferred to Camp Delta where he gave no info. Then taken to Camp X-Ray and put in plywood hut. Interrogators yelled and screamed at him. One interrogator squatted over the Koran.

If you take vengeance on any, take a vengeance proportional to the wrong which has been done you; but if you suffer wrong patiently, this will be better for your soul.

As the subject regresses, his learned personality traits fall away in reverse chronological order. He begins to lose the capacity to carry out the highest creative activities, to deal with complex situations, to cope with stressful interpersonal relationships, or to cope with repeated frustrations.

civilian contractor asked W to come see something. There was an unknown bearded longhaired d gagged w/duct tape that covered much of his head. W asked if he had spit at interrogators, and the contractor laughingly replied that d had been chanting the Koran nonstop. No answer to how they planned to remove the duct tape

Wherefore bear opposition with patience; but your patience shall not be practicable, unless with God's assistance.

The use of most coercive techniques is improper and violates laws.

W observed sleep deprivation interviews w/strobe lights and loud music. Interrogator said it would take 4 days to break someone doing an interrogation 16 hrs w/lights and music on and 4 hrs off.

And be not aggrieved on account of the unbelievers; neither be troubled for that which they subtly devise;

W heard previously that a female military personnel would wet her hands and touch the d's face as part of their psych-ops to make them feel unclean and upset them. W heard that in an effort to disrupt ds who were praying during interrogation, female intelligence personnel would do this

for God is with those who fear Him, and are upright. Whosoever chooses this transitory life, We will bestow on him beforehand that which We please; on him, namely, whom We please:

The torture situation is an external conflict, a contest between the subject and his tormentor. The pain which is being inflicted upon him from outside himself may actually intensify his will to resist. On the other hand, pain which he feels he is inflicting upon himself is more likely to sap his resistance.

occasionally ds complained of inappropriate behavior i.e., incident in which d alleged female guard removed her blouse and, while pressing her body against a shackled and restrained d from behind, handled his genitalia and wiped menstrual blood on his head and face as punishment for lack of cooperation

Afterwards We will appoint him Hell for his abode; he shall be thrown in to be scorched, covered with ignominy, and utterly rejected from mercy.

As soon as possible, the "questioner" should provide the subject with the rationalization that he needs for giving in and cooperating. This rationalization is likely to be elementary, an adult version of a childhood excuse such as:

1. "They made you do it."
2. "All the other boys are doing it."
3. "You're really a good boy at heart."

But whosoever chooses the life to come, and directs his endeavor towards the same, being also a true believer;

loud music and strobe lights

the endeavor of these shall be acceptable unto God.

Jonathan May grew up in Zimbabwe as the child of missionaries. He lives and teaches in Memphis, Tennessee, where he recently served as the inaugural Artist in Residence at the Memphis Brooks Museum of Art. In addition, May teaches writing as therapy at a residential facility for women with eating disorders. Read more of Jonathan's work at his website, memphisjon.wordpress.com.

This poem was previously published online by *Writers Resist*.

How the first strangers met the coast guard

By Arturo Desimone

The maritime guards stopped the half-naked,
very tall animal-headed strangers
on their boats
Asked them "Show your papers, please"
"All we have
are these roses.
Yellow and red
given to us, a gift,
they were once showered upon us from the earth
shot from the first catapults, made to launch pure prayer,
to the clouds fecund,
seeds hit us in our faces, wounding our sleep
The throwers expected our thanks.
Flowers were carried to our mouths in our sleep
by the bearers, hoping
flowers of inedible gold would not descend back
that the shadows of the roots
would end in us."

The guards brandished their weapons, lifting them from the hilt
guns shone like their aerodynamo-sunglasses,
shaven human heads dulled,
touch-screens of their phones bright, all iridescences worn
by opaqued minds of gendarmerie.

"It could be done without any weapon, muscle of titanium tin ton
and iron,
muscle of love-borne waxwing-wind
without any of you enacting vapid designs
or tinkering, in defiance of us
and our plans for your present
and future omni-mud" the gods went on

"Remove the animal masks please" asked the police academy justice
officers,
interrupting, calling in the higher-ranking managerial levels
of divisional security
and other devils that trample the waves and extolled winds.
They phoned them in
on their pink plastic hand-held radios.

the gods answered—But these are our faces.
Only angels tear off their own heads
Every morning, when it is cool they do it down by the lake

Arturo Desimone, an Arubian-Argentinian writer and visual artist, was born in 1984 on the island of Aruba. At the age of 22, he emigrated to the Netherlands, then relocated to Argentina while working on a long fiction project about childhoods, diasporas, islands and religion. Desimone's articles, poetry and fiction have previously appeared in *CounterPunch*, *Círculo de Poesía* (Spanish), *Acentos Review*, *New Orleans Review*, and in the Latin American views section of OpenDemocracy. He writes a blog about Latin American poetry for the *Drunken Boat* poetry review.

This poem was previously published online by *Writers Resist.*

Across the Hard-Packed Sand

By Holly Schofield

Kelly, the dispatcher, sent the call my way, but Nick caught it too, so my squad car arrived at the beach parking lot a few seconds after his. We hadn't worked together much, but I'd sussed him out long ago. He wasn't one of the good ones—those were rare—but at least he mostly pretended I was one of the team.

Unless money was at stake, of course. At five hundred dollars a pair, the toe bounty could be a lucrative second income for us cops. By the time I'd slammed my car door, he was racing ahead down the bank, skidding in the loose oyster-shell scree. "Watch your step, Allie," he called back, his voice holding glee along with old-fashioned gentlemanly concern.

"Alaa," I corrected automatically, wearily. He could have pronounced it right if he cared. But if he cared about stuff like that then I wouldn't be running full tilt through the salt grass behind him, shovel in one fist.

The sun struggled through rumpled chrome-colored clouds and winter still clung to the cold foam of the surf. Kelly had described the radar-tracked location pretty well, and it was easy to spot the dull blue of the shattered spacepod, the size of a bar fridge, way down the gray beach near a cluster of seaweed-streaked rocks.

I began to jog once I hit the hardpack. One foot after the other over this seemingly endless stretch of northern Washington coastline. Fleeing from Syria, sliding into America under the wire, becoming a naturalized citizen, qualifying for state trooper, my personal foot race never seemed to end.

And then the Veldars had come.

And kept coming. And coming.

Would there ever be a time that I could just *stop*?

Nick whooped, thin and reedy over the booming Pacific. He'd reached the crash site and was bent over panting, hands on knees. I wasn't even halfway. I slowed, my bad knee flickering with pain, and walked parallel to the line of unidentifiable sludge that decorated the high water mark. No hurry now. I'd lost. And so had the Veldar.

Sunburned cheeks flushed even redder by victory, Nick waited until I approached then pointed behind the largest rock. "Hah! 'Bout time I nabbed one."

The shivering alien, slightly larger than most, squatted in the rock's shadow, its face-tendrils dangling limply below earflaps. Translucent down to lean gray bone, the alien resembled a large jellyfish that had swallowed a miniature Halloween skeleton.

I avoided its eyes and jabbed the shovel upright in the sandy muck. "You win, Nick." One kick with my bad leg and I sent some bull kelp sailing into the water. I told myself it was a relief that this Veldar's life was out of my hands. Yeah, a relief.

The alien raised a stick-like arm toward us and let it fall. Did it know what Nick was about to do?

Nick was walking around the collection of boulders one more time, being cop-thorough. "Yeah, just the one of 'em," he reported and dusted off his pant cuffs. An all-around typical statie, albeit a bit more fastidious than most. His shirt was still neatly tucked despite his run and his fake sandalwood odor indicated extra-strength deodorant.

Huh. Maybe I could work with that.

"Have fun," I said. "Last time I shot a jellyrat this big, the guts stained my uniform. Even dry cleaning didn't get it out." I stepped back, ostentatiously. "I'll just let you get on with it."

He laughed uneasily. "Hey, five hundred dollars covers a lot of dry cleaning. And, remember, you officially caught this case so you get the paperwork. You can't leave until you do the location sketch. Don't try to weasel out."

"Oh, shit, yeah, all those extra forms. Last time, I forgot one for Fish and Wildlife and the captain gave me hell."

He grunted in faint sympathy, fingering his holster flap but not opening it. The Veldar's various cuts and scrapes had left a trail of yellow-tinged slime as it had dragged itself from the spacepod to the boulder.

I snorted, as if it smelled bad, and took another step back.

"I might have a plastic sheet in my trunk." Nick stroked his thin brown mustache.

I heaved a huge sigh, hoping I wasn't overdoing it. "Tell you what. You get the toes, and I'll dispatch the jellyrat afterwards. *And*, I'll bury it. But only if you do all the friggin' paperwork for me."

A jerk of his head. "What, cut 'em off while it's alive? Seems kinda cruel."

"Shift's almost over. You can get to Sweeney's in time for Happy Hour. And it's not like the 'rats feel any worse pain than a cockroach or something." I held my face tight, lifted my black leather shoe and kicked the Veldar in one of its knees, managing to mostly strike the clear rigid joint covering. It must have seen my quick double-blink because it instantly deflated into the muck and moaned like a ghul. I shrugged. "And I'm in no hurry. I don't go to mosque until sunset."

Nick grinned. "Deal!" He drew out his bowie knife and grabbed each of the Veldar's heels in turn, slicing off the bulbous pinkie toes. The Veldar screwed up its many-wrinkled face and flicked its nictitating membranes but only moaned once more. My stomach knotted and I tasted bile but I held it in.

Nick stuffed the glistening toes in a sandwich baggie. "Next jellyrat gets called in, we can do this deal again, if you want, Allie."

"Sure." I began to dig industriously, my shovel sending gray grit, seaweed, and bits of charred wood flying.

He hastily jumped back. "Okay, then, I'm outta here."

Between shovelfuls, I watched him trot away. I'd have to time the gunshot carefully.

The Veldar lay, knees drawn up, elbows jutting, clutching its bowling-ball belly—resembling the malnourished toddlers I'd lived with back in the Turkish camps. Drying gel clung to the two stumps on either side of its narrow feet. Tired, yellow eyes stared endlessly at nothing.

A few minutes went by. Nick should be almost to the parking lot and out of line-of-sight. I drew my pistol. The Veldar watched me carefully.

I aimed straight out into the ocean and squeezed the trigger.

The retort made the Veldar scoot back against the rock. I blinked twice at it, in reassurance. "Hang in there, little buddy."

Communication via blinks wasn't enough for the next stage. I drew out my black-market English-Veldar phrase book and flipped through it. *War. Run. Hide. Enemy.* We humans might not understand the reasons behind other alien races invading the Veldars' home planet, or how the Veldars could keep stealing motherships full of thousands of these spacepods, but we—well, some of us anyway—understood the fallout. In the tent camp in Turkey, Baba had sat me on his lap and massaged my shrapnel-scarred calf muscle as he pointed out words in his little green Arabic-English phrase book. *Soldier. Injury. Lifeboat.*

That memory was all I had left of my father's own journey—he'd died of a heart attack on our second day in America. I thrust away the thought as I finally found the page full of greetings. Now to see which Veldar language of several dozen.

"Tern ka?"

A blank look. So it wasn't Veldar III. I sighed. This could take hours and I didn't have that kind of time. Maybe I should just drag it to the squad car without its consent. Like border guards had grabbed seven-year-old me. Damn it all, anyway! I kicked some more kelp and ran a finger down the page. "Tennin bran?"

One earflap twitched.

Familiar, perhaps, but not its native tongue. I flipped a few pages to related dialects. "Vronah kro?"

The Veldar's cheeks creased in two directions. "Hrran, vo narhh, hrran!" Its opaque organ sacs vibrated in excitement.

Ah, that was it, then. I made a mental note to tell Kelly to tag this one as Veldar XII in the underground database. "Hnnnah kravv voolah" I pronounced carefully. *Worry no more.*

"Vrahhah?" it croaked out. By now, I knew that word by heart in several languages. *Safety?*

"Hrran," I said with as much conviction as I could manage. *Yes.* It was sort of true. Kelly and I, and a few other folks scattered across the Veldars' vast northwestern drop zone, tried awfully hard to make things safer. Sometimes, we succeeded.

The Veldar relaxed back against the rock, letting its tendrils go slack with relief.

The Band-Aids I fished out of my bra helped with the Veldar's oozing abdominal cuts but they refused to stick to the gunked-up sand on its toes. Finally, I gave up and wrapped its feet in evidence bags. "There. Feel better?" I'd tucked away the phrase book so tone of voice—and a quick double blink—would have to do.

It stretched out three bulbous fingers, forming a pyramid. Another gesture I'd learned in the last few years.

"You're welcome," I replied. "Us refugees gotta stick together." I half-smiled, feeling better than I had all day. Hey, maybe I *could* keep on doing this.

A few more minutes of shoveling and I'd mounded a plausible gravesite. Tonight, I'd drive to Everett in my truck with its special compartment and drop the Veldar off at a safe house. From there, it would begin yet another journey. "Here's two English words for you." I pointed down the coast. "Underground railroad."

"Vrahhah."

"Yup." A cold, damp wind had sprung up and the clouds threatened rain. The folding shovel fit under one arm, and I lifted my burden awkwardly with the other, bracing my bad leg against the base of the rock. The Veldar breathed its odor of burnt raspberries into my uniform collar and wrapped warm, slick arms around my neck. I'd have to change shirts once I got to the car but I had a fresh one ready. I was used to that.

I hunched a bit to protect the Veldar from the wind, sucked in a deep breath, and began the long hike to the parking lot.

Holly Schofield's stories have appeared in *Analog, Lightspeed, Escape Pod*, and many other publications throughout the world. Learn more at www.hollyschofield.wordpress.com.

This story was previously published online by *Writers Resist*.

Feminism

feminism: belief in equality of the sexes; on the basis of this belief, the advocacy of women's right to pursue personal, social, economic, educational and political opportunities equal to those available to men

feminist: oh, the many names that fail to qualify

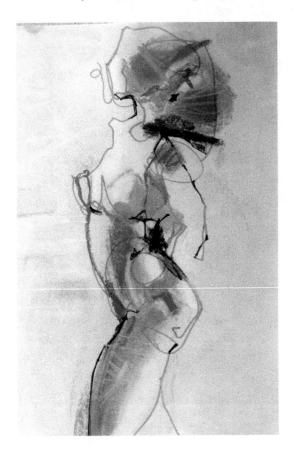

Unchained (11 x 14, mixed media on paper), on the preceding page, is by Elizabeth Jewell. She studied visual arts and literature, taught high school classes in the humanities, then worked at Kentucky Educational Television for nine years. At KET, she developed and taught an on-air class called "Humanities through the Arts." These days Liz marches, writes and works in mixed media.

Resiste / Resist

By Mariana Llanos

Resiste

Resiste, hermana, resiste.
Levanta el puño y resiste.
Resiste, hermana, resiste.
Sube la voz y resiste.
Resiste, hermana, resiste.
Eleva la frente y resiste.
Resiste, hermana, resiste.
Hincha el pecho y resiste.
Resiste, hermana, resiste.
Planta los pies y resiste.
Resiste hermana, resiste.
Entrelaza los brazos y resiste.
Resiste, hermana, resiste
Avanza tu cuerpo y resiste.
Resiste, hermana, resiste.
Con puño, con voz, con frente, con pecho,
Con brazos, con pies, con todo tu cuerpo,

resiste.

Resiste hermana, resiste,

Aunque corra tu sangre

Aunque tiemblen tus huesos

Aunque sangre tu alma.

¡Resiste!

Hasta tu último aliento

Hasta tu último paso

Hasta tu último beso.

Hasta que tu sudor se mezcle en el agua.

Hasta que tu puño brille en el cielo.

Hasta que tu grito se oiga en el viento.

Resiste, hermana, ¡resiste!

Resist

Resist, sister, resist.

Thrust your fist in the air and resist.

Resist, sister, resist.

Raise your voice and resist.

Resist, sister, resist.

Lift your forehead and resist.

Resist, sister, resist.

Bloat your chest and resist.

Resist, sister, resist.

Stomp your feet and resist.

Resist, sister, resist.

Intertwine your arms and resist.

Resist, sister, resist.

Push forward your body and resist.

Resist, sister, resist

With fist, with voice, with forehead, with chest,
with feet, with arms, with all your body,
resist.
Resist, sister, resist.
Even if your blood runs,
Even if your bones tremble,
Even if your soul bleeds.
¡Resist!
Till your last breath,
Till your last step,
Till your last kiss.
Until your sweat blends with the water,
Until your fist shines in the sky,
Until your scream is heard in the wind.
Resist, sister, Resist!

Mariana Llanos is a Peruvian writer and an author of seven award-winning children's books in English and in Spanish. Her first book, *Tristan Wolf*, was published in 2013. Her newest book, *Poesía Alada* (poetry in Spanish for young people) was published in April 2017. She studied Drama in her native Lima. After moving to Oklahoma, she worked as a preschool teacher, standing out for her creativity and passion for arts education. Mariana visits schools around the world through virtual technology to encourage students to read and to spark their love for writing, while building bridges of understanding. Visit her website at www.marianallanos.com.

This poem and translation were previously published online by *Writers Resist*.

Patriarchal Palaver and Politics

By Chinyere Onyekwere

Kpotuba sweated profusely as she climbed the ten dilapidated steps to Nigeria's Independent National Electoral Commission notice board. She looked for her name on the sample ballot, and its absence shocked her, rendering her huge undulating body immobile. She fought back tears of humiliation when a group of certified male contenders snickered as they walked by. Staggering away heartbroken, she flagged down a taxi and wondered what her next line of action could be.

In her bid to vie for political office in her country of Nigeria, the chairmanship post of Achara Local Government Area to be exact, she had unleashed the *Beast*, a deceptive, subtle cankerworm that had been allowed to fester and overrun the district. It marginalized her gender in politics, in virtually all spheres of women's lives. Landmine navigation seemed like child's play compared with her candidacy validation efforts with the electoral commission. The omission of her name from the ballot attested to the well-oiled machinations of the Beast, a calculated attempt to disenfranchise her from the chairmanship race because some of her country's menfolk considered politics their exclusive birthright and domain.

Kpotuba heaved a sigh of exasperation and mulled over her first-time candidature woes as the taxi sped toward her abode. A born leader, Kpotuba burned with passion to make a difference within the squalid environs in which she resided. She organized women groups in her neighborhood, empowering long suffering families to alleviate their poverty-stricken state, a calamitous fallout from economic malfeasance by Nigeria's political class. When the women spurred her to greater heights with a unanimous endorsement for her candidacy, the Beast reared its ugly head.

Unlike her politically savvy male counterparts, she was an unknown quantity, unversed in the art of campaign gamesmanship. When her candidacy was made public, the Beast bared its venomous fangs and sharp talons to bury her long-nurtured garden patch in tons of garbage. Before the effrontery of the assault could be digested, resounding gun blasts erupted in the vicinity of her home—warning shots to scare her out of the race.

They were messing with the wrong woman. The vicious acts had only strengthened Kpotuba's resolve to defy the bunch of desperate, uncouth, rabble-rousing despots determined to derail her political ambitions. Patriarchal marginalization of the female gender in politics was an age-old culture passed down from generations of menfolk to keep women in their place. The Beast held sway in Achara district; women who kicked against it literally battled for their lives.

Even her husband's support was lukewarm. Infuriated, she had rebuffed his salient but ominous "be careful" with silence. Their once amicable relationship deteriorated to an exchange of monosyllables. Her grown children were indifferent, believing they were ignored by a country of failed promises and dubious future, so what did they care? Her political party contradicted its professed motto of equity, justice and peace to treat her with disguised incivility.

Her opponent, Anene Ibezim, the corrupt incumbent chairman

of Achara Local Government Area, belonged to the ruling party. The perks of office lured him to perpetuate himself in power. He ran his campaign by resorting to vitriolic pronouncements with smug certainty of returning to office.

Months earlier, when Kpotuba and Ibezim crossed paths on the campaign trail, he stalked and sized up his adversary with a vow to banish any notions of political exploits harbored by the obese upstart of a woman.

"You'll lose, fat cow," he muttered under his breath.

"What did I hear you say?" asked Kpotuba, stopped her in her tracks by his barrage of words.

"What part of my sentence didn't you understand. Lose or cow?" he asked.

"You belong in the kitchen!" yelled his ragtag entourage before they disappeared into the crowd.

She made an ignominious retreat, but with absolute conviction of his inevitable comeuppance.

When the taxi screeched to a halt, she was jolted back to the present.

The driver demanded his fare, double the standard price. "Why?" she asked, incensed at his belligerent tone. "Because you're double the standard size," he replied, eager to take off.

She alighted from the cab, closed the door with calm exactitude, and paused. A lifetime of imagined and real indignities coalesced into something sinister. She saw a blaze of hot fiery red and lost her head.

Her ensuing scuffle with the cab driver engendered comic relief for Nigeria's pent-up populace; a welcome diversion from disillusion and despair. The fracas drew throngs of people, mostly women who cheered her on. The man, thoroughly terrified of being trounced by a woman, extricated himself from her grasp and fled. She let him escape, had no intention of crossing the thin line between mediocrity and madness to ruin her hard-earned political career.

She dusted herself off with an imperious stance and surveyed the crowd of women whose cries of adulation rent the air when they recognized her from posters advantageously positioned throughout the town. Kpotuba, struck by what could only be deemed divine inspiration, seized the moment with righteous anger to expound on the despicable acts of injustice, meted out to her by the electoral commission.

Her eloquent speech roused the bloodthirsty mob to a fever pitch. Her plight with the Beast became their collective outrage. Like a conjurer's trick, the swelling masses metamorphosed into a full-blown protest march to do battle with the electoral commission's perfidious lot.

Two weeks into the general elections, a political gladiator chose to bedevil Ibezim with a human trafficking scandal that rocked the nation.

Kpotuba won the election—with a landslide—to become the first woman in history to occupy the chairman seat of Achara Local Government Area of Nigeria.

•

A month later, hounded by the Crimes Inquiry Tribunal, Ibezim frantically packed up his personal items from the office. Startled by loud laughter, he reeled around to the menacing sight of a huge body blocking the doorway.

"Goodbye loser," Kpotuba said.

Chinyere Onyekwere is a freelance graphic designer and a self-published author in Nigeria. Her passion for the written word won her Nigeria's 2006/2007 National Essay Competition Award with her story titled "Motion Picture and the Nigerian Image." Chinyere holds a Masters in Business Administration from the University of Nigeria. When she's not glued to the computer screen, Chinyere keenly observes human conditions and the state of the world in general, while trying very hard to not be hoodwinked by her mischievous grand twins. She's currently working on several short stories. You can reach her at ockbronchi@gmail.com.

This short story was previously published online by *Writers Resist.*

familial observation

By Amanda N. Butler

The family
that rallied
against my
first molester
is the same
that voted for
the man
who said
he could grab
me by the
pussy.

Amanda N. Butler is the author of two chapbooks, *Tableau Vivant* (dancing girl press, 2015) and *effercrescent* (dancing girl press, 2017). Her poetry has also appeared in *poems2go*, *Haikuniverse*,

NatureWriting and *ALTARWORK,* among others. She can be found online at arsamandica.wordpress.com.

This poem was previously published online by *Writers Resist.*

Upon Recognizing Yesterday's 'Well-Meaning' Poem Was Still as Paternalistic as Ever

By D. R. James

—1/22/17

Outside, still January, but 40 not 15,
gauzy, black-and-white woods
from *The Wolf Man*. Inside,
a gauzy-gray (un?)consciousness
from *This White Man,* half-reclined
in buttery, dove-gray leather. It's envisioning
millions of protesting women, now back
perhaps in their individual towns,
their power *proclaimed* not awakened,
or still making their way back
from D.C., G.R., L.A., NYC,
Denver, Chicago, Baltimore,
Honolulu, Madison, Wichita,
Reno, Boston, Memphis, Atlanta,
Albuquerque, Gulfport, Asbury Park,

Laramie, Ashville, Orlando, Seattle,
Old Saybrook, Corpus Christie, Erie, Roanoke,
Eugene, New Delhi, Vienna, Minsk,
La Paz, Prague, Strasbourg, Botswana,
EX Village des Jeux Ankorondrano,
Dublin, Athens, San Jose, Sofia,
Copenhagen, Tel Aviv, Geneva, Liverpool,
Cape Town, Moscow, Yellow Knife, Beirut,
Buenos Aires, Belgrade, Bangkok, Boise ...
Will it never, ever learn?

D. R. James is the author of the poetry collection *Since Everything Is All I've Got* (March Street Press) and five chapbooks, including most recently *Why War* and *Split-Level* (both from Finishing Line Press). His poems have appeared in various journals, such as *Caring Magazine, Coe Review, Diner, Dunes Review, Friends of William Stafford Newsletter, HEArt Online, Hotel Amerika, North Dakota Quarterly, Passager, Rattle, The Sow's Ear Poetry Review,* and *Sycamore Review.* His poems have been anthologized in *Ritual to Read Together: Poems in Conversation with William Stafford* (Woodley) and *Poetry in Michigan / Michigan in Poetry* (New Issues). James lives in Saugatuck, Michigan, and has been teaching writing, literature, and peace-making at Hope College for thirty-two years. Read about D. R. James at *Poets & Writers.*

This poem was previously published online by *Writers Resist.*

To the Man Who Shouted "What does your pussy taste like?" as I Ran By

By Courtney LeBlanc

It tastes briny,
like the ocean.
It surges, waves pounding
the surf, punishing
the sand simply for always
being there, for always
being present, for never
leaving well enough alone.

I keep running,
ready to drown him
in a sea of my pounding
feet.

Courtney LeBlanc is the author of two chapbooks, *Siamese Sisters* and *All in the Family* (Bottlecap Press), and she is an MFA candidate at Queens University of Charlotte. Her poetry is published or forthcoming in *Public Pool, Rising Phoenix Review, The Legendary, Germ Magazine, Quail Bell Magazine, Brain Mill Press*, and others. She loves nail polish, wine and tattoos. Read her blog at www.wordperv.com, follow her on Twitter @WordPrev and on Facebook.

This poem was previously published by *Rising Phoenix Review* and *Writers Resist* online.

Miscarriage

By Heather Herrman

A month ago, I lost my daughter to a miscarriage. Science did not tell me she was a girl, but I knew it through every bone in my body. My great-grandmother, Wilhelmina Volk, came from Germany when she was sixteen to an arranged marriage with a drunk. The man gave her two children and then left her. Wilhelmina survived by telling fortunes in the streets of St. Louis. She told them with uncanny accuracy. She saw ghosts of people who'd died across the ocean before ever hearing the news. I claim her intuition as I claim the knowledge of my daughter. She existed. She is gone. This is a truth.

At the hospital, the nurse gave me a pill to expel my daughter's body at home. We knew she was gone because we saw her body in black and blue tones on the sonogram—a little fish who did not move in the ocean of my womb. The tech was cold, ill-equipped to deliver the news.

"There's no heartbeat," she said, after minutes of silent prodding, her hand moving the wand inside of me to send the oh so still image onto the screen while my husband and I watched, breathless. "Let me go get someone," she said.

And that was all. They walked us through the back hallways, so that no one could see us crying. I wasn't crying. I was a farmer's granddaughter. I understood life and death. Cycles. Giving and taking. I was strong.

Stupid.

The tears came later as I paced the house, the pills inserted inside of me to get rid of the dead flesh.

"Like a light period," the nurse told me. "Maybe a little more cramping."

It was a birth. It was labor. I know; I have done it before. I have a son who is alive and well.

I paced the house like a wild animal for four hours, unable to sit, the contractions coming and going, coming and going, the emotions swelling. When she passed, I could not catch her in time and she was gone. Swimming through the toilet and away. Better, maybe, but I would have liked to see her face, the small gumdrop of the unformed woman she might have become.

We do not talk of such things, women. We smile and grit our teeth to the bodily bits of birth. We make pink quilts and sing songs.

And—because we do not speak—it is defined for us by men who make decisions about protecting what is not theirs.

It is mine to give or take. To lose. To grieve or not. It is not yours.

I have deflated slowly, losing the hormones and pounds, letting them push a needle into my arm each and every week to see if my body has stopped its confusion, if it has figured out, finally, that it is not pregnant. It has not. Still, my breasts are tender, my heart is sore. I weep at things that don't need tears. And even more for the things that do.

Around me, the world is falling apart.

And my body aches the ache of a mother.

We are broken, and I don't know how to fix it.

I post the correct posts on Facebook, I speak to relatives in hushed anger about why they must see what it means to let these refugees—these children—into our home, because we are all children. We all ache for a mother.

But I don't know how to translate this white grief into action. I don't know what to do or say that hasn't been said before. I am a pessimist. I am always censoring the personal.

But I like to think my daughter would not. Does not. I like to think she opens her heart and mouth and flies, as Cixous commanded all her daughters to fly, above all this poison through a different language—the language of the body.

The grief of swollen nipples left unnursed, the spread of skin to make a room, left vacant. The body who wants to be made a house.

I do what I have been too scared to do.

I grieve.

My daughter taught me that.

Today, I do not post the protest links on any of the pages where, daily, I make my mask for the world.

Today, I speak from the body.

Today, I speak from the wound.

And with my daughter's voice, which supersedes me, engulfs me, allows me this audacity to claim the universal womb—I beg my children to come home.

Heather Herrman's stories have appeared in journals including *The Alaska Quarterly Review*, *Snake Nation Review*, and *The South Carolina Review*. Her debut horror novel, *Consumption*, is out now from Random House imprint Hydra. Heather has taught writing classes at places such as New Mexico State University, Clemson University, and The Loft Literary Center. She also worked as a literacy advocate at two Minnesota nonprofits before moving to Omaha to birth her were-child and learn the trade of hunting, capturing, and skinning words alive to feed her pages. Visit her website at www.heatherherrman.com.

This essay was previously published online by *Writers Resist*.

The Other Day I Peed on a Stick

By Rae Rose

and when I peed on the stick I knew my blood was like poison.
When I turned 18, I had just started my medication, I peed on a
stick, called a number
from the phone book to see if I could afford an abortion without
anyone knowing.
It was a pro-life group with a deceptive name, the woman begging
me to keep the baby.

So I told my mother. The doctor she took me to stuck his head in
the room, said "Congratulations, you're pregnant." Shut the door.
The woman who filled out my outtake form rattled on about her
midwife. Her face changed. "You're happy about this, right?"
She slowly drew hearts around her midwife's name.

I wished those hearts could work some sort of magic —

make my blood less like the poison I was just beginning to know.
My mother's aunt died of a back alley abortion. My mother wrote a
poem about it called, "Floating," because as she bleeds to death she

is floating above the pain. Or maybe it was the ether that killed her. All sorts of things could kill you from an abortion back then.

At 22 my mother's future mother-in-law said, "I can get you an abortion, but you have to say you're crazy." But my mother wanted him. In fact, my mother has wanted every pregnancy, especially the miscarriage. She has his mobile hanging above her bed.
A group of tiny ceramic bears in bowties that clink sweetly, quietly.

The other day I peed on a stick and when I peed on the stick
I knew my blood was like poison, but without my medication, I'll go crazy.
I'll never be the girl in the movie who throws up, pees on a stick, then says,
honey? I'm pregnant! And runs to her lover. Buys bitty shoes. Buys
bitty hats.

I'll never read aloud to my belly, then deny doing such a silly thing.
I won't look into a tiny face and see a glimmer of me, of my mother,
of my husband.
I won't be looking at someone I will love forever. Someone to give
the world to.
Someone for whom I'd make sure the world was something to fall in
love with.

Trump is the President. I peed on a stick and when I peed on the
stick I knew
my blood was like poison and I'd spare a child all sorts of deformity,
sickness.
I waited the two minutes you have to wait, wondering, what if he
changes everything?
What if someday I can't get an abortion, my blood like poison?

Will we use the phrase "back alley," keep notes for other women of doctors who perform
the operation? Could I become a story my nephews tell? Another aunt with a tragic end? Will I float above the pain? Right out of the world I'd try to make magical for my child
if my blood was nothing, wasn't anything like poison.

Rae Rose is a California poet and essayist whose work has been published in *Cicada Magazine*, *Lilith Magazine* and *The Paterson Review*, among other literary journals. Her book, *Bipolar Disorder for Beginners* is an account, in poetry and prose, of her struggles with that disease. Rae earned her MFA from Goddard College and was the founding poetry editor for *Writers Resist*.

This poem was previously published online by *Writers Resist*.

The Which In Waiting

By R.W.W. Greene

Joanne's television remote hit the wall hard, spawning batteries and bits of plastic that chose their own paths to the floor. She flicked the switch on the power strip that governed the media center and picked up the tarnished hourglass she'd readied before tuning into the ceremony.

Four years would likely be enough, but eight years would be safer. She fit the timepiece into the mechanical hourglass turner she'd ginned up from a junked dryer and set the counter to 70,080. The machine wub-wubbed competently, turning the hourglass end over end over end widdershins. The counter changed to 70,079, then 70,078, then 70,077. … The rig wasn't pretty, but it beat turning the hourglass by hand.

Joanne stifled a yawn. She had time to kill before the spell gelled, and she used it to clean out her refrigerator and haul everything to the compost heap. The rose and blackberry bushes she'd planted around the house were growing fast. Thorns bristled every which way, and the stems were already thicker than a baby's wrist.

Joanne locked her front gate and went back inside to send an email to her accountant.

"Democracy disappoints again, pal. Dropping out for a while," she wrote. "Keep the bills paid, will you? – Jo."

She didn't wait for a response. Tasha Islam had been her accountant for more than a century, and she trusted her. She'd helped set Tasha up in business, after all, and was still her best source for exotic referrals.

Joanne unplugged all of her appliances and took a shower. She brushed her teeth and gargled with Listerine. She browsed Pinterest while waiting for the readout to blink zero, then moved the hourglass to her bedside table. The sand inside glowed like embers. Outside, the bushes finished their expansion, surrounding Joanne's home with a dense wall of brambles and thorns. If that proved inadequate, she also had one of the local dragons on retainer. Joanne rolled a sleeping bag out on the bed and zipped herself inside. The spell took hold, and her pulse slowed. Her eyelids fluttered. Her heart stopped. Her last breath dissipated in the air above her bed, and the dust motes resumed their course.

Time passed.

In Cambridge, a scientist announced a cure for cancer and was murdered in his sleep, his research stolen. A passing meteor resulted in a near panic and the formation of three new doomsday cults. A calf was born with two heads, inspiring yet another doomsday cult. Prince's estate released a new album, "1999 Had Nuthin' on This Party." David Bowie's estate launched his entire catalog—including three never before heard albums—into deep space in search of extraterrestrial musicologists. The polar ice caps melted some more, but no one bothered to measure them. Russia laid claim to East Germany. NASA cancelled the Mars mission: "Too little, too late," a spokeswoman said. A super storm flooded most of the East Coast. The "Fantastic Four" franchise got a fourth failed relaunch. A Cuban upstart claimed to be Fidel Castro in a cloned body and called for a new revolution.

The sand inside the hourglass faded to darkness. Joanne's face screwed up, and she sneezed out eight years' worth of drifting dust motes. Thanks to the Listerine, her mouth tasted fresh, but her body went all pins and needles as it slowly came back to life. When her ability to move returned, she scrubbed at her face with her hands and sat up in bed. Winter light dodged through the bramble wall and trickled through the filthy windows.

When her bedside light failed to switch on, Joanne crooked her fingers to summon a fire imp. The imp darted around the room joyfully, but Joanne halted it with a glare. It settled in the air near the ceiling, flickering sullenly. Joanne got out of bed and tottered on stiff legs to the wall switch. She flicked it up and down several times. Nothing. The imp bobbed, laughing at her. Joanne scowled. Ice on the lines, probably. A storm.

Joanne sent the imp into the fireplace. The dry wood lit with a whoosh, and Joanne fell into the chair beside it to warm her feet. She directed the imp into a lantern on the mantelpiece where it sipped oil and expanded to fill the small bedroom with a warm glow.

Joanne picked the dust boogers out of her nose and threw them on the fire. She'd warm up, eat something, and go back to bed until morning. Prepping the pause was easy enough, but stasis played hell with biological processes. She'd be constipated for a week or better. She rubbed her hands together and pushed them close to the fire. She pulled its warmth into her, using the energy to rejuvenate her groggy cells. She slipped out of the chair and ran through some simple yoga positions before heading into the kitchen for an MRE and a pitcher of water.

In the morning, the electricity was still out so Joanne dressed, grabbed her laptop bag, and went out the front door in hopes of finding an outlet. The brambles creaked away from the door at her touch.

"Hell's bells!" she said. Her garage was gone, as was the car she'd parked inside it.

She turned to fetch her broom but stalled out when she spotted the ragged tents. There were three of them stomped into the snow in her front yard.

"Are you the witch?" said a young woman in a red winter cap, crawling out of her ratty shelter. She squinted at Joanne. "You don't look like a witch."

"I'm no one," Joanne said. "What are you doing here?"

The woman in the red cap looked back at the other women emerging from their tents. "I'm pregnant. They say sleeping here for three days and nights will take away the baby."

The other women nodded.

"That's not true," Joanne said.

"I know a girl wot done it!" said a teenager wearing a hunter-orange snowsuit and a scally cap. "Demon come in the night and took it clean away!"

Joanne sighed. The woman in the red hat was shivering. "Come inside where it's warm at least." She held the door open. "Stomp your feet clean."

Joanne instructed the women from the tents to pile their coats and boots in the hallway and gather in the living room. She summoned another imp for the teapot and set the water to boil. "How far are you along?"

"Six weeks," said Amanda, the woman formerly wearing a red hat.

"Seven fortnights," the teenaged girl said.

"Two months," the third woman said.

"What are your doctors telling you?"

The women looked at each other.

"I ain't seen one, guvnor. Reckon how no one has!"

Amanda shook her head. "Seeing a doctor is a sure route to the breeding camps."

Joanne nearly choked on her tea. "Breeding camps?"

"Aye," the teenager said. "They keep you in chains so no 'arm will come to the baby, miss."

"It's not that bad," Amanda said. "But they do lock you up and watch you for the duration. No smoking. No drinking. No processed food. If you're married, you get to come back home with it. If not—" She shook her head.

"If not what?" Joanne said.

"They take the babe away!" the teenager said. "Send ya home empty!"

"Is this some kind of a joke?" Joanne said. "Did Sonja put you up to this?"

"Sonja, miss?"

Joanne pointed at the teenager, who was warming her scuzzy feet in front of the fire. "Why does she talk like that?"

"*Downton Abby*," the third woman said. She was the oldest of the pregnant tenters, maybe twenty-five. "It's all she's been allowed to watch."

"All I've known since I were a girl," the teenager said. "Like family it is."

"Enough!" Joanne closed her eyes. She extended her senses into the women's bellies and verified the ages of the fetal tissue inside. "None of you want to be pregnant."

The three women nodded.

"And Planned Parenthood doesn't exist, either?"

"We don't know what that is," Amanda said.

"You're all sure about this?"

The women looked at each other for support and nodded.

Joanne concentrated for a moment, whispered a spell, and turned off the fetal-tissues' ability to replicate and grow. It was a simple variation of the spell she used for curing warts and shrinking tumors.

"There. None of you are pregnant anymore. No backsies. Your bodies will reabsorb the tissue. There may be some spotting but—" Joanne dashed into her bedroom and pulled a box of condoms from her drawer. She handed them to Amanda. "Divide these among you. The expiration date has passed, but the stasis spell will have kept them all right."

The teenager held a wrapped condom up to the light. "D'ya eat them?"

"Oh, hell!" Joanne held out her hand. "Give me one of those, and I'll show you how to use it."

"Oooh, blimey," the teenager said after the demo, "I could never use one o' them!"

The woman who was going by the name Amanda but whose aura clearly showed she was lying about it nodded. "It's illegal. My sister had one once. Her husband slapped it right out of her hand."

Joanne summoned another fire imp and took it to the kitchen where she pounded herbs and made up three baggies of loose tea. "This will keep you going for a couple of months. Drink a cup every morning. It's not as effective, and it tastes terrible, but," she shrugged, "it's the best I can do. Come back when you need more."

The women looked at the bags uncertainly.

"You know how to make tea?"

Amanda scoffed. "Of course we do. It's just … we don't have any money."

Joanne opened her front door. "On the house. Once I get the garden going again we can plant enough for everyone."

After the women had packed up their tents and gone home, Joanne headed out again in search of electricity and Wi-Fi. Both were promised at a Dunkin Donuts she found near the highway.

"The sign's not true," the teenager behind the counter told Joanne as she walked in. "We're not hiring."

"I'm just here for coffee," Joanne said. "Check my email."

A pink man in a too-small polo shirt stepped out of the tiny backroom. He pulled the hem of his shirt over his gut. "Who's here?" he said.

The counter girl snapped her gum. "I already told her we weren't hiring."

The man stopped behind the girl and put his hand on her shoulder. "I think you should let me decide that, Jennifer." His smile faltered as he caught sight of Joanne. "I'm sorry." He stammered. "We aren't hiring."

"Just coffee." Joanne held up her laptop. "Maybe a couple of doughnuts and a place to sit for a few minutes. You have that, right?"

The pink man turned red. "Of course." He stepped away from the counter girl. "Jennifer will take care of you."

Joanne gave the blonde girl a friendly smile. 'Small coffee. Black. And two of those chocolate frosteds."

The girl put the doughnuts in the bag, slid the coffee across the counter, and drew her hand away from the $20 Joanne held out. She craned her neck to yell into the backroom. "Do we still take dollars?" she said.

The pink man leaned out of the door without leaving his chair. "What?"

"The old kind of money."

"Sure." He disappeared into the small room.

The blonde girl took the twenty and held it near the register. "How do I enter it?"

The pink man's head appeared in the doorway again. "Convert it to Bitcoin and add four."

The girl did some math. "That's going to be $17.75."

"For a coffee and two doughnuts?" Joanne said.

The girl popped her gum and shrugged.

Joanne took her food and change to a greasy table in the corner of the shop. The coffee was burned and, she soon realized, the doughnuts were stale. She was logging into the Modern Witch discussion board when two overfed cops walked in. Joanne glanced up in time to see the doughnut clerk point her out to them. The biggest one hitched up his belt and strolled over to tower beside her.

"Got a receipt for that computer?" he said.

"This?" She blinked. "It's at least nine years old."

"Where'd you get it?" The cop said. He tucked his thumbs in his belt, thick fingers trailing on the pepper spray looped there.

"Best Buy or something."

The cop shrugged. "If you bought it there, you must have the papers." He looked over his shoulders at the other cop. "They still give receipts out at Best Buy, Nick?"

The other cop nodded. "Last I checked."

"I thought so," the big cop said. "Stand up slow so we can get a good look at you."

Joanne held her hands away from her body as she stood. She'd dealt with enough racist cops in the past to know what set them off. She held still while the big cop took her picture with his smart phone. "Give me a search," he told the device. He watched the screen for a few seconds and grunted. "You aren't even in the system, girly. Must be an Illegal. You just climb over the Wall or something?"

"I've lived in this country since before your parents were born," Joanne said.

The cop laughed. "You hear that. Nick. She said—" The big man flopped boneless to the floor, followed quickly by his partner.

Joanne put the doughnut shop's staff to sleep for good measure. She got back online, downloaded her messages, and filled a paper sack with stale doughnuts to feed her pixies. Her broom wasn't comfortable for long distances, but it got her home in a couple of minutes. The teenaged girl was huddled on her doorstep.

"What are you doing here?" Joanna said.

The girl shrugged miserably. "Me dad threw me out, miss. Told him I'd lost the babe an' he dragged me to the door."

"I would think he'd be happy."

The girl wiped her nose with her sleeve. "It were his best friend's babe, miss. Gettin' me up the tree like that were part of their marriage deal."

Joanne's jaw dropped. "Get inside. You are not going back to that house!"

She set the girl up in the spare bedroom.

Joanne returned to her spot in front of the living room fireplace and watched the pixies eat the doughnuts. They'd refilled the wood box while she'd been gone, and the fire roared merrily. Joanne opened her laptop and looked again at the email she'd downloaded. Tasha Islam, fled to Canada and working out of a brownstone in Montreal—she'd moved most of Joanne's money to an offshore account. Sonja Gomez, her best friend in the witch community, deported without a hearing. Drones fighting World War III over what was left of the Middle East and Northern Africa. Martial law in Chicago, Philadelphia, and Detroit. Texas, starving in wake of its Referendum of Independence.

Joanne stared into the fire. Going back on pause would be the easiest thing for her, probably best for the girl, too. The 1920s were great and the 40s had shown a lot of potential, but Joanne had slept through the 30s and 50s without hesitation. It would be easy to do it again, turn the glass and skip the bad years in hopes of better.

The girl knocked shyly on the door and came in. "Do you have a TV, miss. *Downton Abby* is on in a few minutes and—"

"No TV, but there's a full library in the next room." She pointed.

The girl sighed. "I can't read, miss. Guess I'll just try to sleep."

"Can't read?"

The girl shook her head. "Never went to school. Me dad said it was for boys, no use for a girl like me."

Joanne rubbed her forehead. "What's your name?"

"Zoey, miss."

"Where does your father live, Zoey? Describe it to me carefully."

Maybe this time, better years needed a little push. There were more witches out there, many of them likely on pause but many more just hidden away and riding it out. She would find them. Organize them. There were, no doubt, plenty of girls like Zoey, too. The witches could swell their ranks in a few years, sharing their arcane knowledge with a new generation of women.

Joanne listened to Zoey's description of her father's home and rehearsed her dragon-summoning spell.

R.W.W. Greene is a New Hampshire writer with an MFA that he exorcises/exercises regularly at local bars and coffee shops. He keeps bees, collects typewriters, and Tweets about it all @rwwgreene.

This short story was previously published online by *Writers Resist.*

deity's daughter

By Nikia Chaney

memories are
like the ringing
of bells sharp
bells she
hangs on
the trees
on the hair of her
little girl the little
girl who
shakes her
braids to feel
cool beads
bang on the ear
the shoulder
blade we walk
to catch sweat
and dew
in the morning sweat
and salt and warm

cold so the woman
the woman places
the dark blanket on
the curled up child
the child kissing
us with wind and need
loneliness echoing
and losing itself down
the hall all
these stars buzzing
their pools on the sidewalk
a black sidewalk
full of chalk black
buildings scored
in the heart the
braid in her
hair falling
loose how we would
do anything
to give her a world
in which she had
worth and i
remember yesterday
she drew a dandelion
up to the sky
and blew and
blew and we clung
onto skirts
and we learned
to breathe

Nikia Chaney is the current Inlandia Literary Laureate (2016-2018). She is the author of two chapbooks, *Sis Fuss* (Orange Monkey Publishing, 2012) and *ladies, please* (dancing girl press, 2012). She is founding editor of *shufpoetry*, an online journal for experimental poetry, and founding editor of Jamii Publishing, a publishing imprint dedicated to fostering community among poets and writers. She has won grants from the Money for Women Barbara Deming Memorial Fund, *Poets & Writers*, and Cave Canem. She teaches at San Bernardino Valley College. Visit Nikia's website at NikiaChaney.com.

This poem was previously published online by *Writers Resist*.

A Century of Chipping at the Ceiling

By Robbie Gamble

When I was seven years old, my parents escorted me into a room in a retirement home in Carmel, CA, to meet an old friend of the family. She was a slight, elderly woman with a friendly face and a clear strong voice, and she knew how to set a fidgety, slightly precocious boy at ease. We talked for a few minutes about what I was doing in school and the books I liked to read. She shook my hand, and we moved on. There was something about her that was memorable; I couldn't forget her. Her name was Jeannette Rankin, a native of Montana.

Years later I learned that she was the first woman ever elected to Congress. It was 1916, four years before passage of the Nineteenth Amendment, which enshrined universal voting rights for women (Montana was an early state to adopt suffrage). An ardent feminist and pacifist, Jeannette Rankin voted with a small bloc of representatives against entry into World War I, and subsequently lost her seat. Re-elected to the House in 1940, she was the sole legislator to vote against entry into World War II. In and out of office, she fought for gender equality and civil rights for six decades. She said her proudest achievement was being on the floor of Congress to cast an affirmative vote on the original House resolution for the Nineteenth Amendment as "the only woman who ever voted to give women the right to vote."

I'm fifty-six now, and it boggles my mind that I had the opportunity, within my short lifespan, to shake hands with the first woman who ever stepped onto the floor of Congress as a legislator, exactly one hundred years ago. I've thought a lot about Jeannette Rankin during the last brutish election cycle, the prejudice and intimidation she must have endured as the first woman in an all-male bastion, the patience and endurance she needed to persevere in the struggle for universal suffrage, for civil rights, for peace. I look at Hillary Clinton's tortuous campaign, the obstacles and the misogyny that she had to endure, and it seems like this nation, which appeared to be on the verge of electing our first woman to the presidency, has come a long way in the last hundred years, and yet hardly any distance at all. I'm proud and sad and disgusted all at once.

When I stepped into the booth on November 8th to mark my ballot, I was thinking about Jeannette Rankin, and all of us, women and men alike, who got to stand on her courageous shoulders, trying to break up that damn glass ceiling. The ceiling is still intact, but the fissures run deep, and I draw inspiration from her example of chipping away and speaking out over the long haul, not losing hope despite the setbacks of two world wars and countless other abominations, believing that justice and peace and equality will prevail if we continue to work for them.

She once said, "If I had to live my life over, I'd do it all again, but this time I'd be nastier." Let's keep going, nastily if need be, and with determination.

Robbie Gamble is currently completing an MFA in poetry at Lesley University. He works as a nurse practitioner caring for homeless people in Boston, MA.

This essay was previously published online by *Writers Resist*.

New Madonna

By Celeste Schantz

Visiting a gallery of religious art

I can no longer relate to these dusty
framed virgins and whores. Your Madonnas
are too beautiful; poor, pale, mute dolls
propped against empty cerulean skies.

I want to see some new Madonnas. Of the scars,
of the streets. Our Lady of Goodwill, hunched
at the donated clothes bin. Show me
Madonnas of the long dark night. Our Lady

of Trafficked Saints, protector of school girls
stolen on the cruel road to Damascus.
Render me defenders of girls shot in the head
for being girls. Show me the Malala Madonnas.

Take the apple from Eve's hand. She never
asked for that prop in the first place, obvious

as a smoking gun thrust into a pedestrian's hand
as the robber runs away. Feel free

to put that snake away, too. Eve lives with you
amidst earth's clatter, sewage, bullets.
Eve is Sarajevo, Sudan, Syria, South Central L.A.
and Appalachia. I could show you

the bleak chiaroscuro of a sister trudging home
from her second job in night's dull neon; I'd
shade asymmetry and contrast in her unequal pay.
Color it in napalm, cinder, cement. I'd blend

warm color into her skin … give her some sturdy hips.
Ah, men, you should have shown them as real
women. For this hour, this unjust afternoon,
wags on. Eve and Mary, step down

from that cracked canvas. The distant sun
is lowering behind the trees. Go put on something
bright, happy and yellow. It is time, high time
for these weary sentences to be done.

Celeste Schantz's work appears in *Stone Canoe, One Throne Magazine, Mud Season Review* and others. She has studied with authors Kim Addonizio and Marge Piercy, and was a finalist in a worldwide competition co-sponsored by Poetry International, Rotterdam and The Poetry Project, Ireland. She edits *The Thornfield*

Review, which celebrates women authors whose work has often been disenfranchised by the great white male western academic canon. She lives in Upstate New York, with her son Evan, and is working on her first book of poetry.

This poem was previously published online by *Writers Resist*.

Solidarity

solidarity: the unity, agreement, and support that result from common feelings, perceptions and hopes

In the face of oppression, we write, we create, we resist in solidarity.

Stand Unite Fight, on the preceding page, is by Kit-Bacon Gressitt, a haphazard photographer and the publisher and a founding editor of *Writers Resist*.

We the People Who March

By Yun Wei

We walk because that is all to be done
all our bodies can do
when so much has been done to us.

We walk because it's not done: the work
of hands pressed against stone
and monuments, the work that hands must do

when there are no more parts
to assemble, just an endless sorting
of *hows* and *whys*, punctuation marks

that can't contain the content,
as if brackets could stand for windows,
as if a parenthesis could pronounce *justice,*

inclusive, resistance – all the words
we need in stone. (No need to pull down
the monuments: these were already written)

We walk because gravity is sliding past,
because backwards is not a road,
and when the pavement slides too,

and the lampposts and stoplights,
the freeways and ways to freedom,
we will find a rise in morning light

that casts lines as wide as roads
because rising is all our bodies can do
when there is so much to be done,

so much to make bright.

Yun Wei received her MFA in Poetry from Brooklyn College and a Bachelor's in International Relations from Georgetown University. Her writing awards include the Geneva Literary Prizes for Fiction and Poetry and the Himan Brown Poetry Fellowship. Her fiction and poetry have appeared in *decomP Magazine, Roanoke Review, Apt Magazine, Word Riot, The Brooklyn Review* and other journals. For the last few years, she was working on global health in Switzerland, where she consistently failed at mountain sports.

This poem was previously published online by *Writers Resist.*

March Interrupted:
When Plans Go South

By Julie M. Friesen

I'm at the center of the world right now, but soon I'll go far right of center, to Southwest Georgia. My husband has lost a grandmother, and his mother has lost her mother. I need to be there, meaning I can't be here.

After November 8, a groundswell movement has given me hope. Its extent is not apparent to the public yet, as the media is understandably busy covering the agenda of the new administration and the constant provocations of its leader.

Meanwhile, I'm getting invitations to secret Facebook groups. I'm reading the *Indivisible Guide*, that teaches us how to hold our members of Congress accountable. I'm watching grassroots-born rallies mushroom all over the country. I'm overhearing an acquaintance at a party casually mention holding resistance meetings in his living room.

As much as I dread January 20, I look forward to the 21st, the day the resistance moves from living rooms and secret groups to the streets of the nation's capital. I want to be there to make the statement that we will not sit casually by while our rights are infringed—and not just women's rights, but First Amendment rights, Voting Rights, and Equal Protection rights.

We don't approve of the discourse, especially that taking place in 140 characters. We don't approve of the advisors or Cabinet nominees. We don't approve of the proposed legislation. We don't approve of the bizarre flirtation (and fear the possible collusion) with Vladimir Putin. We don't approve of the ethics conflicts that are being minimized or outright ignored. We don't approve of the attacks on the press. Or Muslims. Or immigrants. Or women. Or Black people. Or people with disabilities. Or the LGBTQ community. Or individuals like John Lewis.

We're here, too.

Instead of marching in D.C., I will be driving past fields dotted with cotton and Trump-Pence signs. After the funeral, I'll sit with my in-laws, who voted for DJT, watch Fox News and bite my tongue raw. But, though I can't be at the march, it still gives me hope to know that our freedoms of assembly and speech will be vividly on display. This time, I'll put my voice on the page. Next time, I'll take it to the street.

We have a voice so long as we exercise our right to use it. And that can be done anywhere, even in Southwest Georgia.

Julie M. Friesen is a lawyer in Baltimore, Maryland, and a writer in her living room.

This essay was previously published online by *Writers Resist.*

In the Trump Era, Factory Workers Send Secret Messages

By Amy L. Freeman

resist

Last Thursday, I found that single word scrawled in black Sharpie on the cardboard inside a package of photos I'd ordered. Odd, I thought, turning over the first of my photos.

The pictures were of me with my children, holding signs at the 2017 Women's March, smiling and determined amidst a sea of humanity. I glanced again at the word. Was it intended for me? Vendors don't send secret messages to customers. And photography places aren't supposed to look at the content of what I've ordered, are they?

I lifted the second pile of photos—me with my children at the March for Science, still smiling, still determined, still amidst a sea of humanity—from a second piece of cardboard. There, in the same hand, another word:

persist

Okay.

Got it.

The words were for me. A photography company's employee whom I'd never meet had probably broken corporate policy in sending them.

Why, though?

When I was in maybe third grade, a teacher assigned our class to create messages in bottles. We were to take glass bottles, decorate them brightly, write our messages on scraps of paper, stuff in the messages in and seal the bottles as cleverly as we could. I used melted wax, rubber cement glue and a top coat of clear nail polish. On a subsequent field trip, we would toss them off a boat and wait to hear back.

Alone in my bedroom, I had written my message. In the quiet of the night, as I pictured the stranger who would find my bottle, the note was more than a school assignment. I looked out my window at the vast darkness, the far-away stars, the scale of the universe dwarfing me. Torn from my heart, my message was a plea to the unknown:

Hear me. Let me know you're out there, too. I don't want to be alone.

That stranger would read my message. Without even knowing me, they would care.

Weeks went by, then months. No one ever replied to my message-in-a-bottle and I eventually forgot about the whole exercise.

That is, until I opened the package last week, when I was suddenly again nine. Except that now, I can see what I could not, then: The power of the exercise wasn't in the anticipation of an answer but rather in the hopefulness of casting my words out to the universe. The act of writing my message, of fantasizing that someone might find it, of knowing someone could find it, was connection enough.

In that spirit, I'm not going to try to find out who sent me the note from the photography place.

Maybe I'm not even supposed to.

I read that employee's message, and without even knowing them, I care. Today, alone in my study, I'm typing this message. It's to you. *Hear me. Let me know you're out there, too. I don't want to be alone.* Resist. Persist. Connect.

An attorney by training, Amy L. Freeman has a day job working with people suffering homelessness. By night she writes. Recent works have appeared in *The Washington Post*, *The Huffington Post* (featured content), *Dogs Today UK* and more. Visit her website at www.AmyLFreeman.com and connect on Twitter: @FreemanAmyL.

This essay was previously published online by *Writers Resist*.

resistin'

By Maia Antoinette

back when hair wove into maps stars aligned as compasses songs
instructed directions and nights moved into risks. since the dawn of
white men in the Holocaust of Slavery Black bodies have refused to
become the livestock of the new land finding liberation in their
transatlantic freedom. since the day that white men decided that
brown people would work on the graves of brown people we sang
our hymns of woe hoping that one day
they would go deaf

Maia Antoinette is a 22-year-old writer, painter, and poet. She lives
in the city of McDonough, Georgia, and is currently an English
major at Georgia State University at Perimeter. She is passionate
about the political and social stances of feminism and Afrocentricity;
the emotional liberation of being secure in one's sexuality,
masculinity and femininity; and self-confidence.

After Charlottesville

By Nancy Dunlop

And may one be
happy in the face of bad things?
And may one make
art or knit or bake a bundt cake in the face of bad things?
And may one have a hopeful
meditative life, a restful prayer life, an active inner life in the face of
bad things?
And may one laugh, make jokes in the face of bad things?
Is one allowed to have a sense of humor,
keep her charming, darling self alive and thriving,
in the face of bad things?
And may one take a walk, looking at the princely tops of
the white pines, remembering
the bald eagles over the lake, bulleting across the sky,
instead of reading another
article, another perspective, another call
to action, in the face of bad things? Is one
allowed to delete the emails screaming
"URGENT! We need YOU more than ever!

We haven't heard from you, in a while. LOOK
at what just happened, NOW."
May one skip the upcoming March Against Whatever-It-Is-Today because
she is tired, just
tired. And distressed by all the distress. Just for today,
may one keep her
dental appointment, go about her business, hold on to that
deep and abiding
crush on George Harrison in the face of bad things?
May one let down her guard in the face of bad things and feel safe
doing so?
Or how about this:
Can one be outraged, scream, hurl
curses like fire balls from her mouth, be a dragon and a good person
all at once?
And while we're at it, can one feel
simple, straightforward outrage, all the while knowing she has
privileges others do not?
Is one allowed to own her fury, even with her blind spots?
Or how about this, and this sounds dangerous: May one just let things
be, in the face of bad things?
May one seek silence for a little while, without
feeling complicit in enabling bad things?
May one feel love for some very specific reason or person or animal
or love
for no reason at all, in the face of bad things?
May one maintain a sense of wonder in the face of bad things, a sense
of yearning, of
eros, of beauty too large to encompass, in the face of bad things?
Can one hear past the static of bad things? See past the constant
interruptions of bad things?

May one write poems
about, say, one's mother, or that young grackle at the feeder, which have
nothing to do with some kind of bearing witness to bad things?
Is one willing to be censured
but speak up anyway in the face of bad things?
Is one willing to make a fuss at a quiet dinner party
in the face of bad things?
May the poet claim oracular sanity in the face of bad things? May she
say, "I see you,
more than you see yourself"?
May she see what she sees and say, "This is my truth and it is valid"?
Is one willing to be yelled down
by a cop in the face of bad things? Is one willing to be shoved
to the pavement? To be imprisoned for pushing back in the face of
bad things?
Is one brave enough to put the sign back up
at the end of the driveway
in the face of bad things?
May one not smile back, although she was groomed to do so,
in the face of bad things?
Is one allowed to dance for two hours a day
in the face of bad things? Or pet the cat, losing all track
of time?
Can one maintain her mental fortitude, her faculties, her intellect,
her sense of purpose, of moral compass, her connection to Source
in the face of bad things?
Does one need to forgive one who does bad things
because she senses he hates himself?
May one just avoid the one who does bad things?
May one simply trust that there is a very large God, a larger
reckoning, which will take care of the one who does bad things?

May the poet do her job, surveying the Universe, swooping into
galactic wormholes, caves of newly formed words, like spores, waiting
to be plucked at their most pure?
May one just. Just just just watch
the new family of grackles whooshing
by the kitchen window, and, not even thinking about bad things,
consider how different she is from them, and how
much the same? How it's all about
wing power?
Can one say to herself, I am an Artist, capital "A,"
and that matters most right now, and mean it? Really
mean it? Believe it?
Believe that is enough? Believe
that Art is what is needed more than
anything in the face of bad things?
May one hold a pen in one hand, a sword in the other and still
recognize herself?
Or is one given the wisdom to know
what to hold, when to hold it, when
to hold on, when to loosen
her grip and stop
just stop
thinking
that she must embrace
all the suffering in this bruised world, just stop
assuming that is, somehow, her job,
a joyless one, a dark and lethal one.

Is there joy seeping out, seeping out, seeping not weeping? Is joy
still there, waving to us, in full sight?

Can one feel joy despite
Joy despite
Joy despite
Joy despite

Nancy Dunlop is a poet and essayist who resides in Upstate New York, where she has taught at the University at Albany. A finalist in the AWP Intro Journal Awards, she has been published in print journals, including *The Little Magazine, Writing on the Edge, 13th Moon: A Feminist Literary Magazine, Works and Days,* and *Nadir,* and in online publications, such as *Swank Writing, RI\FT, alterra, Miss Stein's Drawing Room, Truck,* and *Writers Resist.* She has forthcoming work in *Free State Review* and the anthology *Emergence,* published by Kind of a Hurricane Press. Her work has also been heard on NPR.

This poem was previously published online by *Writers Resist.*

Beware a Kinder,
Gentler American Fascism

By David L. Ulin

Let me begin with an admission: I don't know how to write about this. I've been trying since Wednesday morning, day after the election, when I awakened with what felt like the worst hangover in the universe—and without the benefit of having gotten drunk. I've tried writing about Harvey Milk and the effect of the White Night Riots on the movement for gay rights. I've tried writing about vote tallies and the Electoral College. Tuesday night, I spent half an hour on the phone talking my son off the ledge—or no, not off the ledge, since it was the same one I was standing on. Later, I walked my daughter home from our polling place, where she had spent the day working and had voted in her first election; as we neared our house, she turned into my shoulder and burst into tears. I don't want to make this personal, but of course I do. All politics is personal, or grows out of personal concerns. I am the father of a gay man and a straight woman, and both are at risk today. If you don't think this is personal, then you better get out of my way.

I am not an activist, I am a writer. But we are all—we must be—activists now. As to what this means, I don't yet know. Yes, to protests; yes, to registering voters and contesting elections; yes, to believing—to continuing to believe and fight for—this fractured democracy. But even more, I want to say, a yes to kindness, a yes to the human values for which we stand. This week, I began to dismiss my classes with a wish or admonition: *Be good to each other and be good to yourselves.* They're scared. So am I. It seems the least that we can do.

What astonishes me is that the world continues. What astonishes me is that life goes on. What astonishes me is that I can step outside at break of evening, dusk deepening like a quilt of gauze across the city and everything looking as it always has. Down the street, a neighbor walks her dog while chatting on her cell phone; the smell of wood smoke lingers in the air. Just like last week, just like normal, although what does normal mean anymore? We have an anti-Semite as advisor to the new president, who is promising a first wave of deportations immediately after Inauguration Day. And yet, what frightens me is that in a year, or four months, this election, this administration, will become normalized, as will whatever happens next. We will get on with it, we always get on with it, but I don't want to get on with anything. The dislocation is maddening: the inability to imagine a return.

I'm writing from a place of privilege; I understand that. I am a straight white male living in a (relatively) progressive state. Still, let's not be fooled about what this means. Hate speech in a high school classroom in Sacramento, a gay man struck in the face in Santa Monica. Objects in the mirror are always closer than they appear. I have relatives who chose not to vote for president in Pennsylvania. In *Pennsylvania*, where the final margin was 68,000 votes. If this is a Civil War, it is one in which the battle lines are not the Mason-Dixon line but the driveways that separate us from our neighbors, our place in line at the supermarket, the traffic light at the nearest intersection, the kid at the next desk in our schools.

What do we do about it? We stand up, vocally and without equivocation, for the most targeted and the most vulnerable, we give our money and our comfort and our time. We are still a nation of laws, with a Constitution, and an opposition leadership. This, however, cuts both ways. If fascism or autocracy takes root here—and the seeds have already been planted, let's not delude ourselves—it will be a kinder, gentler fascism, couched in the rhetoric of the American experiment. *Normalized.* That's the America Philip Roth describes in *The Plot Against America*, in which Charles Lindbergh wins the 1940 presidential election and brings fascism to the United States. Roth's country is one in which the World Series is still played in October, and kids sit in the kitchen with their mothers, talking about what they did at school. "Do not be taken in by small signs of normality," Masha Gessen wrote last week on the blog of the *New York Review of Books.* "…[H]istory has seen many catastrophes, and most of them unfolded over time. That time included periods of relative calm." All the same, Gessen reminds us we must "[r]emember the future. Nothing lasts forever." To forget the future is to give up hope, and hope is our most prevailing necessity.

And hope, I want to say, begins with each of us. And hope, I want to say, begins at home. I keep thinking of Vaclav Havel, that dissident turned president, who in his 1978 essay "The Power of the Powerless" stakes out the position of a "second culture," in which freedom begins as a function of our willingness to behave as if we are free. What makes this essential is its insistence that we are accountable, that the reanimation of "values like trust, openness, responsibility, solidarity, love" falls—personally, individually—to us. Keep the record straight, in other words, bear witness and participate, but also hold onto yourselves. "Individuals," Havel writes, "can be alienated from themselves only because there is something in them to alienate." I make a choice, then, not to be alienated; I make a choice to engage. I make a choice to preserve the values of tolerance, of love, of looking out for the other. I make a choice to act as a human being. "If the suppression of the aims of life," Havel continues, "is a complex process, and if it is based on the multifaceted manipulation of all expressions of life, then, by the same token, every free expression of life indirectly threatens the post-totalitarian system politically, including forms of expression to which, in other social systems, no one would attribute any potential political significance, not to mention explosive power." This is the resistance I am seeking, this is the revolution we require.

At heart here is a different sort of normalization—the normalization of who we are. We live in a country where we've been told (are being told every day) that we don't belong. What do you think hate speech is? An attack on our right to consider ourselves American. I am an American, however, and so are you ... and you and you and you and you. I do not walk away from that. We—and by that, I mean we in the opposition—are a nation in our own right and we have to stick together, to find the necessary common ground. My mother, who turns 80 in a couple of months, told me the day after the election that she had been talking to a younger friend, a woman with a teenage daughter; "I won't live to see it," my mother said, "but you and your daughter will." She was referring to a woman president, but also, in a sense, to the restoration of what let's call American values, for want of a better phrase. The conversation made me sad, and yet we can't give in to sadness; that is not our luxury. At the same time, it is also necessary that we express it, that we can tell each other what we are feeling, how we are.

So how are you? I am worried, I am angry, and (yes) I am sad. I am also trying to live my life. This is the normalization I will not yield. Call it second culture. Call it whatever you like. I am reeling, we are all reeling, but I am teaching, I am writing, I am trying to take care of those I love. Saturday evening, I went out for dinner with my family. We sat across from one another and tried to be in each other's company, which remains, as it has ever been, its own small sort of grace. The following morning, my wife and daughter began making plans to go to the Women's March on Washington. This is where we are now. This is who we are. Resist. Remember. Stick together. *Be good to each other and be good to yourselves.*

David L. Ulin is a contributing editor to Literary Hub. A 2015 Guggenheim Fellow, he is the author, most recently, of *Sidewalking: Coming to Terms with Los Angeles*, a finalist for the PEN/Diamonstein-Spielvogel Award for the Art of the Essay.

This essay was previously published online by *LitHub* and *Writers Resist*.

Pride

By Lisa DeSiro

the Aging Bisexual insists his ass is still tight and invites everyone to touch it
the Military Gentleman takes off his shirt and explains his tattoo and weeps
the Lesbian Artist describes the found objects used for her installations
the Fabulous Host kisses guests both male and female on the lips
the Funny Guy imitates his mother's Boston Irish brogue
the Drag Queen hands out cocktails and condoms
the Straight Girl mingles and listens and thinks
no one can tame these lions roaring
laughter spilling drinks filling
bodies dancing music
playing loud and
proud

Lisa DeSiro is the author of *Labor* (Nixes Mate, 2018) and *Grief Dreams* (White Knuckle Press, 2017). Her work is featured in *Nasty Women Poets: An Unapologetic Anthology of Subversive Verse* (Lost

Horse Press, 2017) and *Thirty Days: The Best of the Tupelo Press 30/30 Project's First Year* (Tupelo Press, 2015), as well as in many journals. Her poems have also been set to music by several composers. Lisa lives in Cambridge, Massachusetts, where she earned her MFA in Creative Writing from Lesley University. She works for a nonprofit organization and is an assistant editor for Indolent Books. In her previous career she was a professional pianist. Read more about her at ThePoetPianist.com.

This poem was previously published online by *Writers Resist.*

Standing Rock, 2016

By Marydale Stewart

I sent my heart, that figurative muscle,
that metaphor, that emblem,
to go in my stead to Standing Rock

where my feet have never known the steady earth,
that certain sky, the remembered places the wind has been,
where I've never known another living being as my own,
where the people came together
building, feeding, singing, hoping,
where grief and hope called them all together,
where they're showing a nation how to be a nation.

I've been to other places where the land I stood on
spoke to me with a blackbird's call, a silvered silent creek,
where I sheltered in the humming wind for days, nights,
and the long singing years.

Helpless I am in love and grief,
for the earth is my home, wherever I am.

Marydale Stewart is a retired English teacher and librarian. She has a chapbook, *Inheritance* (Puddin'head Press, Chicago, 2008); two poetry collections, *Let the Thunder In* (Boxing Day Books, 2014) and *Risk* (Kelsay Books, 2017); and two novels, *The Wanderers* and its sequel, *Leaves of the Linden Tree*, both from Black Rose Writing, 2017 and 2018. She also has poems in many literary magazines.

This poem was previously published in the 2017 "Refugees and the Displaced" edition of *DoveTales, Writing for Peace,* and by *Writers Resist* online.

Women in Parking Lots

By Sara Marchant

My hands were full in the post office parking lot. I held out-going bills, my car and postal box keys, my purse, and a heavy manila envelope containing a manuscript destined for greatness (one can always hope, right?). When I heard a loud car horn and a male voice yelling "Votes for Trump!" it was awkward to turn and look over my shoulder.

But we live in times when a male yelling and a horn honking in a government building parking lot signify danger. This might be Southern California, blue state, home of Kamala Harris and Jerry Brown, but my town is rural, poor, and red with baseball caps and Trump bumper stickers—and my mother always preached situational awareness to her daughters *and* sons. So, being a Jewish woman of color, I stopped to locate the danger.

What I saw was an old, fat, cotton-headed white man hanging out of his truck's window and gesticulating with one hand as he worked the horn with the other. He was parked illegally, across three spaces, and he continued to lean on the horn as he yelled out the window. "Votes for Trump! Votes for Trump!" Honk, honk, HONK. He seemed pleased that everyone stopped, turned, and stared. He yelled louder.

One woman did not stop. A small woman, not as old as the yelling fat man, but at least twenty years my senior, she was still moving across the hot asphalt. She wore a turquoise blue, Mexican-embroidered shift and sandals. I'd have admired her dress but I was already admiring her stamina. For she kept walking, even as the man continued his harassment, and it was obvious that she was his primary target. The rest of us in the parking lot were standing and staring, but she kept her back to him. She just kept walking.

She was halfway to where I had stopped when her hand rose over her head. The honking paused for a moment as her fist unclenched. When her fingers folded and the middle finger shot up, up, and up, the yelling renewed and intensified. Laughing, I headed down the sidewalk to join her, and walked with her to the post office door. I held the door open for her. She nodded thank you regally and entered the building, her hand descending to her side.

"What was that?" I asked.

"My friend's husband likes to tease me," she said. "At least, he calls it teasing. I call it something else."

An older woman was sorting her mail at the counter. Her long gray hair was unkempt, she wore a shabby t-shirt over hot pink spandex pants. The stack of mail at her elbow threatened to slide to the floor. My new heroine in the turquoise dress addressed this bedraggled lady.

"Your husband is harassing me again. This nice lady stopped because she was worried about me," Turquoise Dress Lady said.

Pink Spandex Lady turned wearily from her task, and peered around her friend's shoulder to speak directly to me.

"I'd like to put a bag over his head and beat him to death."

She wasn't joking. She wasn't smiling. She wasn't making light of her friend's harassment at the hands—and horn—of her husband. She was obviously tired, hot and too fed up to prevaricate.

We were all women in the post office lobby that afternoon. We were alone with no one to censor us, and she paid us the compliment of speaking her honest truth. She wanted to put a bag over her husband's head and beat him to death. I paid her the return compliment of accepting what she desired in silence. I bowed my head, nodded, and walked away as the two friends huddled in conversation. Before I left the building, however, Turquoise Dress Lady shook my hand in thanks, and we wished each other luck.

That night, when my husband and I recounted our day as married couples do, I told him about the man in the parking lot harassing Turquoise Dress Lady. I told him about her silent middle finger response. I told him about joining the lady in her walk for safety and solidarity. I told him about the wife who wanted to put a bag over her husband's head and beat him to death, and then I started to cry.

I had to explain why I was crying over a stranger I'd met in a post office and a type of situational awareness that I couldn't even imagine. I couldn't imagine sleeping every night next to a man I wanted to beat to death. I couldn't imagine being that woman.

I couldn't have imagined any of what took place in that parking lot, that post office lobby. But it happened. It happened because these are the times we live in.

Sara Marchant received her MFA in Creative Writing from the University of California Riverside-Palm Desert. Her work has been published by *Full Grown People*, *Brilliant FlashFiction*, *The Coachella Review*, *East Jasmine Review*, *ROAR*, and *Desert Magazine*. Her essay, "Proof of Blood," was anthologized in *All the Women in My Family Sing*. Her novella, *Let Me Go,* was anthologized by Running Wild

Press, and her novella, *The Driveway Has Two* Sides, was published by Fairlight Books in July 2018. Sara's work has been performed in The New Short Fiction Series in Los Angeles, California, and her memoir, *Proof of Loss,* will be published by Otis Books in their 2018/2019 season. She is a founding editor of *Writers Resist.*

This essay was originally published by *Roar: Literature and Revolution by Feminist People* and *Writers Resist* online.

A Drill Song from the Turkish Resistance

Translation by Süleyman Soydemir and the Turkish Youth

From an anonymous variant of a military drill song, "Gündoğdu Marşı," or "The Sunrise Anthem," was a symbol of the anti-fascist Turkish resistance in the 1960s and 70s. Today, it serves as a symbol of hope in the face of an increasingly authoritarian regime.

Gündoğdu Marşı

Gün doğdu, hep uyandık
Siperlere dayandık
Bağımsızlık uğruna da
Al kanlara boyandık

Yolumuz devrim yolu
Gelin kardaşlar gelin
Yurdumuz da faşist dolmuş
Vurun kardaşlar vurun

Yurdumuz da faşist dolmuş
Vurun kardaşlar vurun!

The Sunrise Anthem

At sunrise, we all wake up
Trenches bracing our shoulders
For our freedom we stand against
Blood-red shrapnel showers

Our path leads to revolution
March on brothers and sisters
Against this fascist infestation
Strike on brothers and sisters

Against this fascist infestation
Strike on brothers and sisters!

Süleyman Soydemir, who lives in Turkey, is a believer in the supposedly antiquated chants of Liberty, Equality and Fraternity, and he is a student of Anatolian Folk Traditions and Culture. His current—and perhaps ultimate—purpose in life is to tell the stories of resistance against tyrants, thieves and internet trolls.

This translation was previously published online by *Writers Resist*.

Pain

By Katie Thomason

I'm in my favorite bathtub, once my escape pod. This cold, white, cracked heart of my home is far from luxurious. It's an antique porcelain tub with rust around the drain. No claw feet or sloping sides. No jets or built-in seats. It's my favorite, because it holds me and gallons of warm water and it's my retreat from pain.

I'm always in some level of hurt. My neck is jacked up. The final straw hit my already fragile cervical spine when I was teaching high school. I got new students with two or three weeks left in the school year. They had been expelled from other schools and had nothing to gain or lose. I was trying to power through end-of-year, high-stakes testing with students who had been with me from the beginning. We were tired. The new students had defiant energy and jumped all over my weaknesses. I broke. That was years ago. Now I have a disability check, a half-written novel, and lots and lots of baths.

All the numbered Cs in my spine have permanent issues. The angriest C, C-4 I think, likes to pinch the nerves that shoot spikes down my left arm. But all my Cs are screaming pissed off. The best way to get them to chill is to soak them.

But as the warm, soapy water relieves my physical pain, my mind winds up. It's as if my head waits for my neck to shut up so *it* can start bitching me out. Flashes of failure plague me. It starts with every mistake I've ever made, every injustice I've faced, every drunken humiliation. No amount of dunking my head under water will quell this.

I get that physical pain exists to tell you something's wrong, but there's nothing I can do to fix the underlying problem and make it stop. The problem is with the signal light itself. It won't stop flashing.

That's also true of the increasing mental pain.

It's not the fight with a co-worker from three jobs ago, missed deadlines, mistakes in front of classrooms, or my wife's failure to hang towels correctly. In the last year or so, it all hurts much more than usual, and the battles are terrifying. Now it's like the mental pain is stronger than the physical, making all of it worse.

Pain now stems from one source. Just like the news and late night comedy, my baths are all about Donald Jackass Trump. Rusty bubbles of putrid bullshit surround me. I am now reliving clashes fought with flat screen political pundits or people I barely know on Facebook: *Watabouda Dems16, Sacred Semiauto, 1Ad Hom Eminem.*

Worse, people I've known and trusted my whole life are now defending this man's hateful rhetoric.

Friends I went to choir practice with: My marriage will hurt society, but old, rich-man adultery is cute.

The class clown from high school: Teachers get paid too much; they should be security guards, too.

Friends who drove trucks with Confederate flags taped to the back windows: Being American means standing ovations for the president.

Friends I once trusted with my secrets and insecurities are now standing with the playground bully. They point and laugh at my United States. *My* U.S. used to be better than this. Sure, she's a privileged kid who makes lots and lots of mistakes and even bullies people herself, leaves a trail of native tears, kills black babies in their grannies' backyards, dishes out justice on slanted scales. But *my* U. S. was trying to make amends, learn from her mistakes. She let me marry my love, who leaves crumpled towels on the floor.

Now, everyone seems to want to take the U.S. back to her darkest hours, the same ones they call *great*. If greatness comes at a hefty price others have to pay, I call it *hate*, not *great*.

And the hate seems stronger than me and my crooked neck. I can't defend my lovely U.S. Sure, she eats too much fast food, pops pills, talks trash, and smacks her chewing gum, but she sings beautifully. Her voice is rich and layered and full of heart. What can I do, a floating mass in a bathtub scrubbing between my toes? I am ill-equipped to protect anyone, and I've sloshed too much water out of the tub.

I'm getting cold. I throw open the hot water and yank my foot from under the faucet with a new shock. It's as if I forgot it would be hot. I purposely put my foot back under the rush. I won't acclimate, if I don't embrace the heat.

I've spent too much time shrinking from it—ignorance of my country's ignorance was bliss. Knowledge is searing pain.

I used to teach my students knowledge is power. Now, I think of the high school students and teachers who are no longer stressed out by high stakes testing or going to a new school at the end of a year. The ones who died. The ones who survived, they thought they would be supported in wanting to make their schools safe again—make our country safe again. But that support butts up against the greed agenda. I can learn from these students. They carry a painful knowledge, but they are far from powerless—the pain empowers them.

I rise up. My sharpened Cs yelp. I don't acknowledge their bullshit. I drain the tub and step out, dripping onto the floor. I pick up a mostly-fresh towel, dry off and neatly fold and hang it back on the rack.

My bath time has dulled my body's physical and emotional noise, but not shut it up completely. That's good. No, it's great. I will use it. I will learn from Parkland high school students. With my body, I will join the marches. My tired, disabled body will be counted. With my mind, I will write and resist and shout so the values of *my* U.S. are heard. With my spirit, I will fight for the embattled soul of the United States. Fueled by my pain, physical and emotional, I know there is no retreat. I will not give up.

Katie Thomason is a Los Angeles-based writer obsessed with Appalachia, but not enough to move back in with her parents. She holds an MFA in creative writing from the University of California Riverside, Palm Desert.

Nuestra Música / Our Music

By Sima Rabinowitz

Nuestra Música

Hay silencios sagrados
las pausas frágiles entre palabras

Hay silencios desgraciados
quedarnos mudos cuando hay tanto que exige expresión

Hay silencios inesperados
ya no recuerdo el timbre de tu voz

Hay silencios desanimados
tener que repetir una vez más nuestra petición

Hay silencios que insisten
que resisten
que saben salvarse

Hay silencios que son como museos
archivos de almas desvanecidos

Hay silencios que sueñan
con una noche—una sola noche—sin tiros

Hay silencios que inventan su propia historia
para no dejarnos sin narrativa

Hay silencios que inspiran
una íntima benedición tentativa

Hay silencios que hacen una tregua con la noche
ocultando sus motivos

Hay silencios que nos dan la fuerza
de seguir siendo testigos

Hay silencios robados, fallados, falsificados

Hay silencios engañados, lastimados, dañados

Y hay silencios que ruegan ser llenados
de un canto humilde de amor

Our Music

Some silences are sacred
the fragile pauses between words

Some silences are disgraceful
we are mute when there is so much to say

Some silences are unexpected
I no longer remember the sound of your voice

Some silences are weary
having to repeat our request, once again

Some silences insist
some resist
some know how to save themselves

Some silences are like museums
archives of vanished souls

Some silences dream
of one night—just one single night—empty of the sound of gunfire

Some silences invent their own history
so we won't be left without a story

Some silences inspire
a tentative, intimate prayer

Some silences call a truce with the night
hiding their motives

Some silences give us the strength
to carry on serving as witnesses

Some silences are stolen, mistaken, false

Some silences are deceptive, damaged, injured

And some silences beg to be filled
with a humble song of love

Sima Rabinowitz is the author of *The Jewish Fake Book* (Elixir Press) and *Murmuration* (New Michigan Press). Her prose and poetry have appeared recently in *The Saint Ann's Review, Amp, Hamilton Arts & Letters*, and *Trivia: Voices of Feminism*. She wrote "Nuestra Música" for her dearest friends and her community in the Bronx.

This poem and translation were previously published online by *Writers Resist*.

Say It Aloud

By Jamie Davenport

Something entirely disturbing happened last night on my commute to rehearsal. Bear with me. It is a long tale. But one that is necessary to read and digest.

I was sitting in the corner of the Red Line T, closest to the conductor, when a group of about eight black kids from the ages of 12 to 16 entered.

I automatically noticed their presence because of how loud and rowdy they were being. Smiling at how crazy they were all acting, I turned up the music in my headphones and bounced along with the train.

I noticed the boy sitting across from me. He'd entered the train with the other kids, and although also black and about their age, he clearly did not know them. From his body language it was obvious he desperately wished he had sat in another section.

At around the South Station stop, the conductor's door swung open, and through my oversized headphones I could tell she told the kids to quiet down. The kids mouthed off to her and she called the MBTA security.

At this point my headphones are off and I am listening with full intent. The MBTA guard, a white man, walks on and within ten seconds announces that he is calling the police and that the train will not move until they come. He is greeted with a resounding, "Are you kidding me?" from just about everyone on the train.

I automatically zone out and think about what I was doing from 12-16.

I think about breaking into my old elementary school and stealing ice cream.

I think about joyriding my boyfriend's lifted, bright green, Chevy blazer without a permit or a license.

I think about getting caught drinking in a friend's backyard.

I think about trespassing on private property and swimming.

I think about getting pulled over twice in the same month, on the same road, in the same place, by the same officer, in the same car, for the same reason, and waltzing away from the scene with nothing. And I mean nothing, but "a get home safe."

I think about every single actually illegal thing I have ever done and realized one harrowing fact:

I have never been touched by a police officer.

I have never been handcuffed.

I have never been to jail.

I have never even gotten a ticket.

I have never left an interaction with the cops with anything other than a "have a nice night."

I wake up from my reverie and we are still parked at South Station. I tune into the conversation around me and hear the kids. Let me emphasize *kids*. Kids making a game plan for what they will do if the police start to shoot them.

I glance up at the boy across from me. He is squirming. He wants off. He is texting fiercely. I'm assuming he's telling someone what we are both observing.

The girl next to me notices my presence and says,

"Sorry for messing up your ride."

I say, "Don't worry about it."

My voice catches on the last word. My throat starts to sear.

She asks, "Are you upset?"

I respond, "Yeah, I guess I am. I just don't understand why they are calling the cops."

She says, "Because we are black."

The 12-year-old turns to the group and quietly says, "Black lives matter."

They all murmur in agreement.

The police arrive and everyone remains very calm. Eerily calm. Everyone is walking on eggshells. The cops step on the train and tell the kids if they get off quietly they can get on the next one and go home. The kids accept the offer and begin to clamor off. At long last the boy across from me and I are left alone.

As I begin to put my headphones back on the police reenter the car. They look at the boy and say, "We said everyone in the group has to get off."

The boy says, "I don't know them."

The cops say, "It's an order. Everyone in the group has to get off."

I jerk a little, as if to collect my bags.

The police look at me and one says, "Not you. You're not in the group."

The policeman places his hand on the boys shoulder and guides him toward the door. In a moment of temporary rage blindness I stand up and scream, "He doesn't know those kids."

The cop looks at me and says, "Is that true?"

To which I say, "Yes, and it was true when he said it, too."

The police release the boy and he sits down across from me again. We share a moment of blankness and then tears well in my eyes.

He waves me over to the seat next to him. He says, "That was because I am black, wasn't it?"

I nod. He looks down sheepishly at his shirt and says quietly, "I'm just happy they didn't hurt me. That would kill my mom. And she is not someone you want to mess with."

I say the only thing I can think of. "I'm so sorry."

He says, "With all that's going on in the world, I am so scared all the time."

We sit in silence for a moment and I decide to change the subject. I ask him about himself. He tells me he is entering his junior year of high school and spending the summer working for an organization that aims to help people learn how to have healthy relationships. He says he wants to help stop domestic abuse. He tells me he is passionate about gender equality. He asks me if I know there is a difference between sex and gender. He says he wants to educate the public on that topic.

The train rattles into my station, and I shake his hand. He says, "Thanks."

I mumble, "Don't mention it."

I exit the train and watch it pull away. And then I weep. I weep in a way I never have before. My breath shortens and I begin to crumble.

I weep for Trayvon Martin.

I weep for Mike Brown.

I weep for Sandra Bland.

I weep for Alton Sterling.

I weep for Eric Garner.

I weep for all of the names I do not know but should.

I weep for their families.

I weep for their friends.

I weep for the innocent blood shed all over this country.

I weep for that boy.

I weep that I cannot remember his name because it is not as familiar to me as James or Tim or Dave.

I weep for those kids.

I weep for all of those kids.

I spend the night replaying the whole scenario over and over again in my head, and realize that three words keep running through my mind. Three words that, until I heard a 12-year-old black girl say them aloud to her friends as they awaited the police, I did not understand. Three words that are so little, but mean so much.

Black Lives Matter.

I stop crying. I become resolute. I make a pact with myself to help the world become better for those kids.

I make a pact with myself to spread this story like wildfire.

I make a pact with myself to be an ally to that beautiful boy.

It starts here.

Before you read on make a pact with yourself to join me.

Before you read on commit yourself to this cause.

Before you read on openly admit that racism is alive and thriving in this country.

Before you read on promise yourself you will say the following three words.

Aloud:

Black Lives Matter.

Didn't do it? Here's another chance:

Black Lives Matter.

Still can't say it? Ask yourself why?

Black Lives Matter

Here's another chance:

Black Lives Matter.

Here's another chance:

Black Lives Matter.
Black Lives Matter.
Black Lives Matter.
BLACK. LIVES. MATTER.

Jamie Davenport is a Boston-based writer, poet and playwright. She graduated in December 2015 from Emerson College. Her work has been published in *The Independent* and performed at Arena Stage in D.C. She runs a poetry Instagram account called @davenpoems.

This essay was previously published by *The Independent* and *Writers Resist* online.

Flood, Fire, Mountain

By Liz Kellebrew

Flood

That morning I climbed out of bed and watched my neighbors. They rowed away in a boat launched from their porch. When I went downstairs, water bubbled under the carpet like boils. My Christmas tree lay on its side. No one bothered to knock on my door.

Fire

"Don't shoot," he said. They shot anyway. After he died, the fires burned all over Ferguson. And they spread, the country a furnace of protest. No one bothered to listen.

Mountain

The next winter, I drove through snow banks six feet high under green-blue alpine spruce. A miniature avalanche rolled down before me and I stopped. Because, red fox slender paws golden eyes! Crossing unafraid.

Flood

I sacrificed my precious books to save my one and only couch. Goodbye Tolkien, goodbye Gibran. The waters rose, gaining depth and current. Outside, someone had tied a goat to the bumper of a Land Rover. It wouldn't stop bleating.

Fire

The weekend before Christmas, protestors shut down the mall. Seattle Times, sad children and frowning grandmothers: "Isn't there a better way to get their message across?"

No, no there isn't. This country loves money more than freedom. It won't listen to anything else.

It won't stop the bleeding.

Mountain

In the spring I hiked alone, Sunrise Trail. Wildflowers poked out of mist: Indian paintbrush, foxglove, mountain gentian. When I turned back, surprise! A female elk, my shadow companion.

She walked away, stately, a queen in leather.

Flood

At the Red Cross I stood alone, waiting in line. Families in tents, in sleeping bags, piled in every corner indoors and out. Instant Homeless: Just Add Water. They gave me a debit card to buy food and boxes.

FEMA was clueless. They came four weeks late and wanted to give me a TV to replace the one I never owned.

Fire

The Reverend Jesse Jackson came by my work. I only heard about it afterwards.

The socialist newsletter I subscribe to invited me to a protest.

More children were shot, more unarmed men killed by police.

A week later, there was a bomb threat at work. I only heard about it four hours later, after the SWAT team announced there was no bomb.

Mountain

I put my fingers in the stream, but I did not drink. Clear ice melt washing emerald-gold moss and pebbles in a hundred shades of earth.

The salmon don't spawn here. But sun-yellow butterflies light on the banks with feathery feet, long tongues curling.

Flood

When the water went back to the river where it belonged, blonde shocks of hay hung from power lines like the dried up scalps of Norse giants. Guess we showed them.

Fire

"All lives matter," they yelled. And by "they" I mean the people whose children weren't murdered in cold blood by a standing army. Occupation Domestication. No Voice Without Retribution. No More Constitution.

Silent, it smolders.

Mountain

Granite shoulders like a Picasso portrait, Blue Period. Cloaked with snow, capped with a swoff of cloud, trees at her ankles a golden froth of maple sugar, and that silence— broken! Because groaning glaciers, calving into babbling streams, tumbling into gurgling rivers and crashing into roaring oceans and this whole shouting planet of grasshoppers chirping and elk lowing and coyotes yip-yip-yowling and the fishermen coaxing their mermaids into rainbow nets of desire, because the starlings singing to children in the city and the oaks in Fremont cracking open those sidewalks with their wide black roots bursting out of every confining concrete wall and spilling over to fill the empty spaces left behind—!

Liz Kellebrew lives in Seattle and writes fiction, poetry, literary essays, and creative nonfiction. Her work has appeared in *The Coachella Review*, *Elohi Gadugi*, *The Conium Review*, *Mount Island*, *Section 8*, *The Pitkin Review*, and *Vine Leaves Literary Journal*. She holds an MFA in Creative Writing from Goddard College.

This poem was previously published online by *Writers Resist*.

Impressions of the USA

By Tran Quoc Cong

Tran Quoc Cong paid his first visit to the United States in 2007, a guest at the memorial service for author and Pulitzer Prize winning Viet Nam War correspondent David Halberstam. Mr. Tran had guided the journalist during a visit to Viet Nam and they befriended one another during the author's return visit some years before his death. Mr. Tran was so moved by his invitation to the memorial from Mr. Halberstam's widow, by the opportunity to experience the United States, he kept an email journal of his travels. These email messages from 2007 now serve as a reminder of the country's national character beyond the context of the Trump regime, as seen by a traveller who lived through devastating political turmoil.

Dear Friends,

Good morning, America!

SEAT BELT makes me feel clumsy like spaceman in the spaceship. Trying to remember. It takes some time.

Crossing the streets here is a skill, not an art, like in Viet Nam. Press the button. Magical!

I borrowed a digital camera, but my mind still analog.

In Viet Nam, eat to live. Here, live to eat.

I have a dream. My dream comes true.

Thanks for all your help,

Tran Quoc Cong

Dear America,

Descartes in America: "I DRIVE therefore I am."

You have driving license, you are somebody. You have wings like angels. I feel disabled because I cannot drive. In Heaven, the angels fly, not walk. My mind, eyes, body in Heaven, but I cannot fly, just borrow the wings.

Mr. Don Giggs offers me a car. Just looking, not driving. How can I change lanes? In Viet Nam, the lanes are built-in and invisible. Very happy to see the sign "Drive Less, Live More."

House/home is really a castle, fortress. Cars are moving castles, fortresses on freeway.

Best,

Tran Quoc Cong

Dear America,

You are the XXXL country; your meal is, too. A cheeseburger is so BIG, it swallows me, not I it. If I keep on eating like this, I do not think I can walk through the door at the customs counter with the slogan "Keep American's Door Open and Our Nation Secure" on the day I leave the paradise.

Things are expensive.

In the announcement for the memorial service for Mr. David Halberstam in NYT: "In lieu of flowers, the family asks that donations be made to Teach for America in the Mississippi Delta." Flowers for David, food for me. Teach for America, Teach for my children. Mississippi Delta, Me Kong Delta.

This is an open eyes and mind trip for me.

Thanks for all your help,

Tran Quoc Cong

Dear America,

Memorial Day, Sunday 27 May. Riding bike in Westminster Cemetery, I agree with Thomas Jefferson that "All men are created equal" and buried, cremated equal.

"Flat" means equal in some way, in many ways. In Viet Nam, the graves are not equal at all. In Viet Nam, the hill is for the tombs, death, resting place. Turning your head to the mountain means "pass away." Flat, low land is for villages, life. In U.S., in reverse.

Now, I know why you are "The Quiet American." You do not blow the horns when you drive.

I sleep with the sound of click in my dream. "Click It or Ticket." Seatbelt, please.

See you,

Tran Quoc Cong

Dear America, Good morning, Sun Valley!

Vietnamese local bus from Little Sai Gon to Phoenix, 9 a.m. to 4 p.m. Heaven to Hell. Just hot, not humid, like home. No sticky. Anyway, 5-star Hell. Just compare, not complain.

The pages of my high school textbook, *Practice Your English*, McGraw Hill, appeared along the road. The first time in life I saw desert, cactus, sand, small bushes, hot and dry. Before, I only see dessert, fruits, ice cream, sweets, caramel, after meals. I felt thorny, like cactus when coming to Arizona. Cowboy films 1965 to 67 replayed.

CARPOOL LANE = Mahayana Buddhism. You live, pray, do

whatever to become Buddha, and help the others to become Buddha, too. The other lanes on freeway = Theravada Buddhism. One vehicle, one driver.

In the U.S., I live to be delivered. I cannot drive. Thanks for all help. I come to the U.S. with JFK Inaugural Speech, MLKing's "I Have A Dream," the image of Apollo 11, and all my high school textbook in mind.

It is my America.

Tran Quoc Cong

Dear Phoenix, Arizona,

Wooh! Grand Canyon, Great Wonder of Nature, so grand.

"No one should die before they see Angkor," Somerset Maugham wrote somewhere. To me, "No one should die before they see Grand Canyon." Coming to Angkor, we stretch our necks UP to see how high. To Grand Canyon, we crane our necks DOWN to see how deep. Angkor, the hand of Man. Grand Canyon, the hand of the Creator.

Riding bike in and around Phoenix in June, I know why the Phoenix puts its head in the ash. To hide from the HEAT.

Buying something, I have to pay tax. I feel itchy. You don't, do you? Just the system.

See you,

CONG

Dear Old Town Scottsdale, the West's Most Western Town,

I rode my Iron Horse—bicycle—to the frontier town 113 years after the first settlers came. I met again my boyhood with the cowboy films in my mind, *Arizona Colt, Bonanza, The Wild Wild West.*

I clicked my camera as fast as the sheriff shot his Colt to stop the bandit coming to town.

I pumped air into my bike tyre in front of the Cavalliere's Blacksmith Shop, like the cowboys changed horseshoes.

I locked my Iron Horse at the rusty ring once used for horses and mules.

I sent two postcards home from Scottsdale's first Post Office, where every founding father gathered at mail time, twice a day.

And, I had an ice cream in Sugar Bowl Ice Cream Parlor, to cool down the notorious Arizona dry heat. I am the *Man from Nowhere*. A really good day.

Bye bye, from Where the Old West Comes Alive,

Tran Quoc Cong

Dear South California and Arizona,

Walking in Mission San Juan Capistrano, I saw Silent Night, so quiet.

Standing in front of Crystal Cathedral, I heard Jingle Bells, so loud.

The bronze sculpture of a woman caught in adultery, "Let the one who is without sin cast the first stone." They mean tons, tons of glass of the cathedral, neither Magdalene nor adultery.

Thy kingdom comes. Maybe. Looking at all stuff in the U.S. so far, I have felt the Middle Kingdom comes. Everything made in China, except the Cowboys in Rawhide Steakhouse and Saloon.

How come? Hey, folks!

Tran Quoc Cong

Good morning, New York,

You are Grand Canyon turned downside up.

MANHATTAN, I dropped my HAT 3 times while looking at your skyscrapers, you made my neck painful. I became a MAN without HAT or sunTAN, you are my sunblock buildings.

I saw 3D New York vertically, on Top of the Rock and in subway. First time in my life subway, like guerrilla Củ Chi Tunnels. New

York, you made my provincial heart choke.

Early morning walk in Central Park, the lung of NY. At home, when getting angry at somebody, we shout madly, "You are a dog!" Watching people dog-walking here, from now on, I will not shout like that. It is so nice. Will find something else, worse.

Oh, my God! I said, Oh, my Dog! I heard the echo from the bench behind. You made me confused.

CONG

Dear 13 Original States,

Promenade in and around Brooklyn (Broken Land), Greenwich, East Hampton, New Canaan. I wonder how many Gods you have. Only one, right? So, why you have so, so many different churches? It doesn't mean that you are more religious than us. Maybe less. You make God lose his identity. Holding the banknote, I read "In God We Trust." Singular? Walking around here, I see plurality.

Riding bike around East Hampton and Connecticut is like in the Anderson fairytales. Nice landscape, golden sunshine like honey, green forest, the weather just perfect. I wonder if we need paradise in the next life. God is unfair. Now, I know why you often end your speech, "God bless America." You bribe Him?

Since coming here, I have had the feeling I am spewed out of the Horn of Plenty together with food. How can I control the temptation?

Forgive me,

CONG

Dear New York,

Welcome to Paradise. We know that even Paradise is not perfect. Spewing out of the subway, woo! Times Square, the Crossroads of the World, not easy to cross due to the crowd. Your five senses are raped by the Most Crowded on Earth, the Call of the Wild.

NEW York is new to me, but OLD to the immigrants in the Lower East Side tenements.

GRAND Central Station engulfs you.

GREAT Depression still in some corners I walked through.

BROADway is really broad.

LONG Island is a long drive, just like your common question in Viet Nam: "How long to Ha Long?" So long to Ha Long, so long to Long Island.

Burger KING swallows you like King Kong does.

CENTRAL Park right in the center you never miss.

TOP of the ROCK is top of tops.

SUBways like submarines.

WALL Street is only WALLs and GLASS, which makes the TRINITY church so TINY, so PITY.

TIMES SQUARE is not square, but like the hands of octopus.

HOTline 1-888-NYC-SAFE is extremely HOT at Times Square to fight terrorism.

DEAR New York, you are very DEAR, not cheap to live.

Looking at Lady LIBERTY, I think of Lady Buddha. This with FIRE, that with WATER. Two basic things for life. (Lady Buddha with the flask in her hand pouring water down to extinguish the inferno of our life).

New York, you are XXXL. Forgive me, the frog, for the first time, leaving the pond for the ocean. How can I see you all, let alone understand you?

Take care,

CONG

Good Morning, Washington DC,

The bright sunny day: All the monuments, domes, spires, statues rise up to the sky, soar to the heaven, except Viet Nam War

Memorial. Black, like the pin, goes deep to the soil. The White House is white. The Black Marble is black.

In the morning, coming to National Cathedral on the hill, I do not see God nor congregation. Emptiness.

In the evening, sitting in the baseball stadium, I see the holy congregation. Their religion is Baseball, singing like church choir. Eating and drinking like sharing the Communion. The 12 Apostles down there bring their spirits up to Heaven with Bats and Balls. When a ball flying to the seats, many people rise up trying to get it like holy blessing. At the back, food and drinks are their "daily bread" they pray for. Some people concentrate on the pamphlet of statistics like Psalms. Baseball caps everywhere like halos. Red and white T-shirts for sale like angel robes. Everyone is happy as they are in Heaven. The first time in my life I watch a baseball game right in the Baseball Cathedral.

I have some books on Baseball Saints by David Halberstam, whose death is the Visa for me to be here. Both Baseball Bible and Baseball Service in Baseball Cathedral are completely dark to me. But I enjoy the Touch of America.

Baseball Bless You, America. Baseball is with you, and you with Baseball.

CONG

Dear Philly, good day Atlantic City.

Woo! The Cathedral of Gambling with the double-ten commandments advised by American Gaming Association. Oh, my God. GAMING looks like GAMBLING. This is that. I wonder if caSINo has SIN within itself. Hope not. But I doubt. And I didn't see any SAINT here.

Looking at the stream of people coming, focusing their eyes to the slot machines, I heard the words "free to pursuit of happiness" echoing. Losing, return to win back your losses. A win, return to win more. E-Z Pass. Go faster. Go ahead. No clock. Neither day nor night in casino. No-Times Square.

You are in Heaven with thousands of colorful neon lights, make everything DOUBLE, TRIPLE, One four Four. Ecstasy. Drinks are free and welcome to lure you to the dream of winner. Gambling is GAME and BLIND. Knowing when to stop?

Responsible Gaming means Irresponsible Gambling, doesn't it?

A mime tried to be machine-like. Robot tried to be human-like. Foot Massage and Palm Reading next to each other.

SIN City Mt. Holy Town. The young smile, the old napping.

White, Black, Yellow, Brown skin, the Sun makes all shadows the same on the white sand.

Atlantic City always turned on.

On the drive back to Philly, I saw the sign STAY AWAKE! STAY ALIVE! Otherwise you die. You intend to gamble your life? BOARDWALK is life.

Horn of Plenty.

Food, Fun and Friendliness.

We the People, Pursuit of Happiness.

CONG

Dear Atlantic Ocean,

The first time in life, I dipped my hand into Atlantic Ocean. Just over there is Nantucket, where the ashes of David Halberstam will rest. May my soul hitchhike the ferry across. Should I take some ash and drop it into Me Kong Delta, so he can meet his youth again?

One Very Hot Day. I stopped by the house of Home Sweet Home in East Hampton, and the

birthplace of the author, America the Beautiful in Falmouth.

I walked step-by-step on Boston's Freedom Trail, not crazy rush like on the Freeway.

In Boston, I slept in the bed of a Marine who was moving from Kuwait to Iraq. I saw all his high school and college pictures, books, souvenirs on the shelves.

In Falmouth, I sent a letter to SPC. Johnson Stephen, who was now somewhere in Iraq, telling him about his beautiful Falmouth village, lighthouse, fishing, swimming and wishing for his safe return, not mentioned the bullshit war at all.

During Viet Nam War, at 15, I found many Xmas cards handmade by primary students in the States, in the Rear, sent to the GIs in the Front. Those were my boyhood toys, which I found in the garbage dump near my school.

Goodbye, Boston. Farewell to the navel of American Revolution. My body is in Jacksonville, Oregon, now, digging gold, but my soul still somewhere in New England with golden memories.

Many American-Vietnamese here never touch the navel of U.S. history and Revolution. They just do nails, run barbershops, and mow the lawns, trying to make $$$. Gold Rush no longer rushes. Hair, nails, and grass keep growing. We cannot stop them. The longer they grow, the more $$$ my friends make. Their American Dream fulfilled. The streets are paved with gold.

Up near Crater Lake , the first time in my life, I touched snow. Two little girls threw snowballs to me. I sat and lay on it. I walked, doubting my feet like Neil Armstrong's first steps on the Moon.

Goodbye, Boston. 4 July. I left the Cradle of Liberty, Birthplace of American Independence right on her 231st birthday. I ate hot dogs, potatoes salad, baked beans on the East Coast, and watched fireworks in the West, Oregon.

I am in Arcata, CA now.

CONG

Dear friends,

Good evening America. I set foot in LAX at 6:25 PM 21 May. Like Neil Armstrong stepped out of the spaceship walking on the Moon, like the Pilgrim Fathers landed at Plymouth Rock, I stood in line at Visitors Counter, Customs, at Tom Bradley Int'l Terminal in high spirit of Apollo and Mayflower. I giggled like the angels had the new wings ready to fly in Paradise.

My wife feels proud and happy back home in Viet Nam. At long last, at least once in life, her husband goes to America. The Promised Land, Paradise, Heaven, Something Number One.

She boastly told all the villagers, "My husband saw a pumpkin as large as a house in America." All the villagers listened, mouths and eyes wide open.

Another lady said, "My husband also saw a cooking pot as big as the Village Commune."

How come! What for?

The answer: "My husband's pot is used to cook your husband's pumpkin."

Best,

Tran Quoc Cong

Dear America,

My soul and mind are untidy like NASA in Florida the day Apollo 11 returned from the Moon.

My visit to the U.S. Paradise is the reincarnation to me. I still have East-West jetlag. Climatically, Paradise. Purgatory, jet lag. It is The 0001 Place (not 1000) to see before you die. 101 Things to Do in life. Not many people have their dreams come true in this lifetime. I am one of the few. Out of more than 3000 photos taken during 90 days in the New World, the Dreamy Land, I had to choose the best, iconic 10. And if only 3 chosen, which ones should I pick out? I told my family, friends, neighbors, colleagues what I have seen:

- the button to cross the streets
- the subway in NY and Washington DC.
- the snow in July at Crater Lake
- the Atlantic Ocean
- the Central Park in NY, desert in Arizona, Redwood Forest …

What I have tasted:

- the biggest burger
- the brownie and trail mix
- the blueberry and yoghurt
- the corn and salmon

What in USA scared me:

- I almost burned my finger with the hot water tap in the kitchen.
- the alarm at my classmate's house. He gave me his house key, but his wife set the alarm as usual. I opened the door, and the siren barked fiercely. So scared, I just stood at the door holding my passport, just in case the police came. … Goose bumps. "Ask not what American will do for you, but what together we can do." But, I am alone then.

Yesterday, my daughter asked me if I had any dream, dream to go visit somewhere, somewhere else.

No, I have no dream now. It takes time to have another dream. I feel full, my five senses.

Many thanks, USA,

C O N G

This was previously published online by *Writers Resist.*

CPSIA information can be obtained
at www.ICGtesting.com
Printed in the USA
FSHW01n2236050918
51812FS